To █████████

Thank you fo-r

Richland College has been a

huge support to me & my

speaking journey.

Continue Inspiring others!

'Create Your Future Self'

Victor f

Sept. 2019

Proven Pathways to Wealth and Happiness

♦

Victor Johnson

Published by: TDR Brands Publishing

TDR

ISBN-13: 978-1-947574-06-9

DISCLAIMER: Although the author and publisher have made every effort to ensure that the information in this book was correct at press time, the author and publisher do not assume and hereby disclaim any liability to any party for any loss, damage, or disruption caused by errors or omissions, whether such errors or omissions result from negligence, accident, or any other cause. Additionally, this book is not intended as a substitute for the medical advice of physicians nor the psychological guidance of a psychiatrist. The reader should regularly consult a physician in matters relating to his/ her health and particularly with respect to any symptoms that may require diagnosis or medical attention and should seek professional help related to any mental concerns the reader may have. This book simply outlines the steps that the author personally took to achieve financial success and the results are not guaranteed for anyone else reading this book.

CONTENTS

FOREWORD

Congratulations! I am congratulating you because you are doing something that so many others are afraid to do; you are taking action towards improving yourself. Sometimes, taking the first step is all you need to make life-changing miracles happen. Truth be told, you have already impressed the hell out of me. I'm serious! It takes true courage to make drastic changes that differ from what you were already doing; however, in many cases, these changes are the only way for you to truly see dramatic results in your life. Now, I have a few questions for you.

Are you struggling with your finances?

Do you feel constantly overlooked for a desired position of employment?

Are you constantly playing catch-up with your bills?

Do you feel like you have bad luck?

Do you feel that things simply don't work out in the manner that you would like?

If you answered 'yes' to any of these questions, this book will give you the tools to achieve better outcomes in all areas of your life. Believe it or not, a positive state of mind will fix most of your problems. Your mind contains much more power than it's granted credit for; by planting specific thoughts and visions into your mind, you have the ability to bring those thoughts into being.

Have you ever heard the phrase, "Positive vibes, positive life"? Well, it is true! The most wonderful part about a positive state of mind is that it's available to us all, regardless of race, income level, religion, age, gender, sexual orientation, physical build, or geographic location.

In this book, you will discover specific and powerful actions that will allow you to change your life and set yourself up for wealth and happiness. As a matter of fact, my specific path prompted me to generate passive income via rental properties. In this book, there is a specific section regarding the purchase of my first rental property.

As we study history (and research some of the most successful people within a variety of industries), the application of vigorous levels of thought and imagination for the sake of achievement is a common link. Successful people are not successful because of 'superpowers' or an abundance of resources. As a matter of fact, many successful entrepreneurs in today's society were originally 'broke.' However, the inner voice and/or subconscious thoughts of successful individuals is what allowed them to visualize their winning moments. In order to succeed, we MUST be able to see ourselves in our exact, desired state of being. Throughout my journey, I constantly recited the following affirmations to myself:

"I am successful at everything I do; I am a success; I am a healthy, happy, wealthy, and giving millionaire entrepreneur."

This same phrase is still displayed on my computer screen-saver, my cell phone lock screen, and the mirrors in my bathroom; I constantly read similar statements to keep my subconscious focused on these matters. As the great Buddha once stated, "What we think, we become." Day in and day out, we must train our subconscious mind to direct our thoughts towards our desires. I like the saying, "train your brain."

In this book, I delve into the exact actions and thoughts that I applied to achieve financial success in my life. If I can do it, anyone else can. The point is this: we all have the ability to reach the accomplishments of the greats. In order to do so, we must dig deep within ourselves, set our minds on our objectives, and go after them as if success were our only option.

My only request is for you to truly commit to be the best version of yourself. Believe in the process; know that you are more than capable of becoming your greatest self. Moreover, fight for your happiness and wealth. You (and your loved ones) are completely deserving of financial freedom.

1: MINDSET CHANGE

Have you ever been in a situation where you lost your set of keys? You check the key holder near the door, your purse, and book bag, yet come up with nothing. You ask everyone in the house whether or not they've seen your keys; they haven't. Then you stop, taking time to retrace your steps, and come up with nothing!

If you've ever been in this situation, paused, and repeatedly said, "I am about to find these keys," you may have suddenly looked at the sofa and seen a shimmering object. Viola! Your keys are under the sofa pillow and close to a piece of mail. This exact situation has happened to me. I stopped panicking, took a deep breath, and told my subconscious mind, "I will find these keys." Since my subconscious mind is the dictator of my thoughts, my inner talk put me in the position to successfully locate my keys.

The makeup of the subconscious mind is loosely designed like the mainframe of a computer. In layman's terms, the subconscious mind will do whatever it is trained to do (void of any emotion or logic). The user is the one who determines the results of their experiences; if he or she is careless and attempts to override the design of the computer, it will lock or display the 'blue screen of death.' The subconscious mind also operates in this manner. Your subconscious mind operates from your experiences, knowledge, visuals, and interactions. Your conscious mind, on the other hand, operates according to your emotions, external influences, and internal interpretations.

Therefore, if you tell your subconscious mind, "This will not work out because it never does," the subconscious mind will believe this affirmation and ensure its exact outcome. Due to the nature of the subconscious mind, we must educate ourselves and move in the direction of our desired outcomes. One of the best ways of doing this is by planting seeds into your subconscious mind multiple times each day; doing this will mold the seeds into real results.

This process is just like working out; greater amounts of arm curl repetitions increases the strength and size of your arm. After a while, people will notice your frequent arm curls even if you are not holding a dumbbell; it will simply become part of your normal existence. However, if you stop doing those arm curls after a few compliments, your arm will slowly regress back to its previous state. In the worst-case scenario, your arm could become flabby and weak. Your subconscious mind should be viewed in the same manner.

The daily habits and mindsets that are required to conquer obstacles in the path of success are the reasons why millionaires are millionaires. Wealth and happiness are ongoing journeys, not specific destinations. Once you decide to adopt a mindset of success, wealth, health, happiness and freedom, this mindset will become part of your existence for the rest of your days. Once you have established this mindset, you will then have the responsibility of passing that wisdom on to someone else who needs it.

Let's go through a quick exercise to prepare you for the mindset shift that you are about to experience.

Find a quiet place in your home, preferably a place where you can sit or lie down for 10 minutes without any interruptions. This may be the hardest part of the exercise for some of you. If it is, go out to your vehicle (or even out on the porch) and take a seat (as long as this place is quiet and free of disturbances.)

Once you have found this place, take a seat (or lie on your back) and close your eyes. Begin to inhale and exhale, deeply and slowly (take four seconds to inhale and eight seconds to exhale.) Do this five to ten times in a row. After you have completed the breathing exercises, keep your eyes closed and say: "I AM HAPPY, I AM HAPPY, I AM HAPPY," while smiling. Repeat. **Really believe in your soul that you are happy!**

The point of this exercise is to prompt your acknowledgement of the word *happy*. Say it as often as you can so it becomes a familiar term. Saying and hearing the word has its own power; this simple exercise puts your mind 'on notice' that you are in charge and ready to take your mind in a new direction. Get yourself ready to experience happiness on your terms. Also, please understand that this exercise is not an overnight process. It will require hard work, dedication, sacrifice, and even some moments of frustration; however, you must remember this: *you are in complete control of your thoughts!* Protect what gets in there by keeping as many positive, success-filled thoughts in your mind as possible. Place reminders in places that you will find them; this will allow you to have constant reminders of the happiness that you will achieve.

> ## LIFE COACH MOMENT
> You are awesome! You really can do this!
> You are stronger than you realize!

The fact that each and every person who walks the Earth is in search of happiness has always fascinated me. Since the beginning of time, happiness has been hunted by every man and woman and in every corner of the world. Even though we all are searching for this one thing, happiness has a trillion, gazillion different looks, feels, tastes, and meanings. So, what is the meaning of happiness? Per Dictionary.com:

Happiness – (Noun):

1) The quality or state of being happy

2) Good fortune; pleasure; contentment; joy

Wow – those definitions are beautiful! Although, what they don't tell you, is that reaching this 'state of being happy,' particularly on a lasting and ongoing level, can be quite stressful. Throughout moments of our lives, we all have experienced great joy. Obviously, happiness means different things at different stages in our lives; we all know the joy of playing with our children, kissing our significant other, or winning a competition.

On a financial level, you may have received an unexpected raise or worked hard for overtime pay on your check causing the extra time to REALLY pay off. Those things are awesome and will continue to happen; however, for one moment, I want you to imagine a life that allows you to experience those joys every day when you wake up and go to sleep. Imagine a life of calmness and relaxation without a 'financial' issue that you're unprepared for. Claim this reality today!

> ## LIFE COACH MOMENT
>
> Stop holding onto things that are holding you back. It could be a possession, a person, or a bad memory–LET IT GO! Don't let your past live in your future. Imagine how proud you will be to look back at these things to see how far you have come! You are stronger than you realize!

Do you want to be a millionaire?

According to *Business Insider*, "The number of millionaires in the U.S. has hit an all-time high." They go on to publish, "Credit Suisse says 1.1 million new millionaires were created in the U.S. in 2017. That brings the total number of millionaires in the U.S. up to approximately 15,356,000, or about one in every 20 Americans" (Holodny, 2017).

Look at that; you have a shot! In fact, you have much more than a shot; you have just as much intelligence as some of these millionaires, and more intelligence than some of the others. Make it happen, Captain!

My mother reminds me of a time when I was seven or eight years old. During this time, I randomly turned to my mother in her car and said, "Ma, I'm gonna be a millionaire one day." My mother, being like most mothers, looked me in my eyes and said, "Jabo (my childhood moniker), you can be anything you want to be." That was really all I needed. Throughout my life, I have been able to approach most situations with a positive mindset; this positive approach has paid me huge dividends, which included pretty good jobs, good fortune, and meeting the right people. My only struggle was managing the money that I was earning. In my early 20s, I got a job as an account representative for a small collection agency in Norcross, Georgia.

During this time, the agency was collecting Southern Bell phone bills that were past due. In this role, I earned a base, hourly pay, but the job was all about making your bonus check as big as possible at the end of each month. All of the heavy hitter account representatives were upstairs. The entry-level representatives were on the first floor, but I knew I needed to get upstairs as quickly as possible. So, what did I do? I decided to find an upstairs mentor who could teach me the ropes. At 22 years old, I also decided to dress and present myself 'as if' I were already working upstairs and making those huge bonus checks.

Within 60 days of my hire date, I was moved upstairs and given my own file to work from. During the first 30 days, I generated a bonus of about $500; this was great for me, but the heavy hitters were earning north of $2,500 each month. I continued listening to the experts, talking to my mentor, dressing well, showing up early, and staying late (when I was allowed). Within three months of my $500 bonus check, I was consistently earning $2500+ in bonuses each month. That was game-changing money for a 22-year-old who was living in a small one-bedroom apartment, with two young children by two different women. The bonus increases allowed me to be a more supportive father to my two young children and I was able to do more exciting things. Notice I did not say anything about saving money or paying off prior debts.

Even though I was earning this extra money, somehow, I was still always broke before my next payday; bonuses were only paid once per month. This cycle of getting paid, but not paying all of my bills in full each month, landed my credit score below 600. Moreover, my blind ambition as a young man prompted me to start a couple of businesses even though I did not understand business taxes.

Therefore, I ended up with a couple tax liens on my credit, which lowered my score to 550 or so. There I was, a young, healthy, ambitious guy making good money, yet I still had horrible credit and no real financial plans. Many of you can relate to this, which is why I am writing this book. I want to help you focus your mindset on the elimination of debt, the diligence of saving, the courage of investing (so it grows), and living a happy life for the rest of your days.

2: LAW OF ATTRACTION

By now, you may be getting the theme of this book: if you control your thoughts, you control your life. It is important to be protective of what you focus on because these are the things that you will attract. The universe is a huge ball of energy that circulates everywhere; it sways in the direction of the energy around it. If there is negative energy in the atmosphere, all the things circulating around this atmosphere will be negative. The same principle applies for positive energy; it attracts more positive energy. This is not a new idea. For many centuries, philosophers, educators, scholars, doctors, neurologists, and others have tested and retested this theory, and, each time, they came up with the same outcomes. Like attracts like.

Medical and neurological evidence supports this theory. On the website of Law of Attraction, the following key points resonated with me: 1) the power of positive thinking has support within the medical communities, and 2) neurologists understand and know that visualization can help create a better future.

One prominent example of scientific support for the Law of Attraction was published in the *Yonsei Medical Journal* in 2007. Korean researchers Ji Young Jung et al. found that there was a strong connection between positive thinking and overall life satisfaction in the population, which echoes the sentiments of scholars who suggest positive thinking exercises as a way to boost manifestation potential. As the authors of the medical journal article noted, "These findings offer promise of positive thinking as an approach for psychological interventions designed to promote life satisfaction."

For point two, scientists working at the Welcome Trust Centre for Neuroimaging at the Institute of Neurology in London have discovered that people who visualize a better future are more likely to be able to bring that future into existence. This, of course, is just what the Law of Attraction tells us—that daily, vivid mental images of a better life help to draw that life towards us. In the publication documenting their findings, the neurologists wrote "The ability to construct a hypothetical scenario in one's imagination prior to it actually occurring may afford greater accuracy in predicting its eventual outcome."

You get what you focus on, so focus on what you want. Continue speaking, thinking, and believing that you already have what you desire and let it gravitate to you. Words have meaning. Furthermore, it is not your job to figure out exactly how your plans will come together; your job is to put the best plan together, maintain positive thoughts, and let the universe handle the rest. The thing is, we do not really know how everything comes together; it could be something that happens to the friend of a friend, thus prompting your good fortune in a situation. How could you possibly know what goes on with someone whom you do not know? You couldn't, yet it could still positively impact your outcome. Your positive thoughts draw positive outcomes to you. For this reason, I have made a habit out of reading things that attract positivity, abundance, good health and love to myself and my loved ones. I do this each day just before going to bed and shortly after waking up. It's gotten to the point where I just read various positive affirmations throughout my day; I do this at my desk before I start working. I do this as I take a brief walk outdoors, when I start the Jeep at lunch, while on the treadmill...anywhere!

Creating vision boards is one of the other things that my wife, Latasha, and I have both started doing. Vision boards are just that, a board on which we stick pictures of our dream destinations, vehicles, homes, health, and other goals. This gives us an exact image of the things we are visualizing for our future. Now, I have them at my desk, on my bathroom mirror and in my phone. All these things may seem fanatical to some readers, but if you are serious about your goals and dreams, these are small sacrifices for a better life. You will have your desired result once you grasp the concept that a happy life requires small, daily lifestyle changes. None of the aforementioned exercises required me to spend any money or do any hard labor.

Here are examples of how the law of attraction works: we all have experienced moments when we have thought about buying a new vehicle, considered a certain make and model, and then, all of a sudden, three of them drive by. Perhaps you were humming a song in your mind and then it suddenly played on Pandora. There have been times when I started thinking about someone I hadn't seen in ages, then suddenly I get a call or a text from that person within a day.

This is all energy. Trust me; it is not just a coincidence. Now, as we implement this process for our larger goals, you must also believe that it is possible. You can cancel out those positive vibes with just one negative thought of disbelief. If there is any doubt in your mind that your larger goals are not possible, your subconscious will say it must not be possible.

Be confident; know that it can and will happen for you. Why not? There is no reason. Go after your dreams with passion and enthusiasm. You will be highly rewarded for your trust. In most of the jobs that I worked, especially in the earlier stages of my career, I imagined myself being in the role of my boss. With true dedication and vision, I would study as much as I could regarding the company's business. Sometimes, I would be given an opportunity to step in as a 'substitute supervisor,' which gave me a chance to see things from the boss's vantage point. I used all this information to consistently become the top performer on the team. My bonuses increased, but more importantly, I was promoted when opportunities appeared. That mattered because I wanted to add those experiences and job titles to my resume and LinkedIn profile. By my mid-20s, I was in a lower management role, but I was managing. This was only within two years of when I first started dressing like a boss and acting 'as if' I were the boss.

Visualization had a lot to do with my ability to consistently advance, and it required a good attitude. Most of the people who know me personally and professionally will probably describe me as a decent guy who does what he can to help people. For that, I thank my deceased grandmother, Pearlie Mae Anderson. She raised all her children and grandchildren in a somewhat stern manner, but always taught us to be good to other people. Helping people and having a good attitude has drawn many blessings my way, from small yet important ones to large and life-changing ones.

When you visualize your outcomes, really try to be in that moment; imagine what you would wear (exact outfit or style), the scent in the room when you are offered that promotion, or how the conversation would go. When your mind has a true image of that successful moment, the mind knows the moment is possible. The more you feed your mind with those types of thoughts, the more it will attract similar experiences into your life and guard against anything that opposes the visualized outcome. Work hard to conquer negative thoughts about money, people, and things. Focus on things that will promote your spiritual, financial, physical, and mental elevation. It takes a lot of energy to hate someone or something and it drains our life. That energy should be redirected towards prosperity - you must not waste this energy.

Over the past five years or so, I have taken this mentality to an entirely new level. Because of this mentality, I have been able to attract higher paying jobs, eliminate all $25,000 worth of debt, and save and invest lots of money. With precise accuracy, I am now able to dial into specific goals and watch them manifest. Although I would be foolish to sit here and tell you that this was all done by my excellence, I give all credit to God who has given me this amazing ability to use the laws of attraction and universal energy to achieve most of the goals I have accomplished. I carry myself with an air of gratitude because I realize that God has placed certain people and situations in my path, and I have been able to remain awake during those encounters.

That awakening has led to the happiness that I have always wanted. Do not neglect the spiritual presence in your life (whatever it is for you). We all need a spiritual base to establish a sense of morality and to give us unseen strength to take us through the tough spots that life presents us. For a while, my wife and I served within our church in Smyrna, Georgia; however, in 2013, I accepted a job that moved us to Texas and we never really found a church home after that. What I can tell you is that my bond with God and my desire to serve others have never wavered. This lesson was taught to me early on; I have embraced the attitude that if I continue to be of service to others, the universe will always take care of my needs. You can count on that. God and the universe depend upon all of us to find ways to help the less fortunate. This is even more rewarding when we do so without expectation of some favor in return. Do good because the universe is good to us; doing so will always ensure that the energy that you put out, comes back to you multiplied. Whether or not that energy will be positive or negative is your choice.

You may want to implement the following action items to help you make a mindset adjustment:

- **Create a Vision Board**. A vision board is an inspiration board that reflects the things that you want in your life over the next two years; maybe it has a picture of the exact house you've been driving by and really want for yourself and your family. Maybe the vision board has a specific position at your current place of employment (or a different one) that you are pursuing. The board can also include a picture of a car, a dollar amount you want to see in your bank account, or even certain number of rental properties that you want to acquire within the next two years. Don't FEAR adding things to this board just because you don't know how they will be accomplished. This board is only designed to document your dreams. The loftier your vision, the better.

- **Write Down Positive Affirmations**. Find a mirror, wall, or door that you walk by multiple times each day and write down five 'I AM' statements. Things such as: "I AM HAPPY," "I AM WEALTHY," "I AM HEALTHY," "I AM PROPEROUS," and "I AM SUCCESSFUL." These affirmations should be written in big, bold letters and appealing to the eyes. Place the affirmations in the location of your choosing and read them aloud at least three times on a daily basis. The most important time to read them will be just before you go to sleep and as soon as you wake up. Doing this will help your subconscious mind absorb these thoughts as your reality.

- **Write Down Three Things You Are Grateful For**. This is very important; it will help you appreciate what you already have, even if it may have lost value in your eyes. This can be a significant other (or loved one), a vehicle you currently drive, a job you have, or a home that you are in. Although you may want to upgrade some (or all) of these things, for now, you must appreciate having them. Perhaps these things bring you varying degrees of stress; however, looking back, are they better than what you had previously? Maybe or maybe not; it doesn't really matter. This exercise will help you show yourself (and the universe) that you are ready to receive more of these great things with more abundance and happiness tied to them. Sometimes, we forget just how good our current state truly is. Of course, we would like better things, but we should also be thankful for what we have. Someone out there has far less than you and would be happy to achieve your status within the next two years.

- **Smile.** Smiling is an open expression to the world around you; smiling tells the world that you are happy, at least in the given moment. Smiles also attract more smiles and cause people to view you as open to new opportunities, conversations, and more reasons to smile. Science has shown that the mere act of smiling can lift your mood, lower stress, boost your immune system and possibly even prolong your life. According to an article by Nicole Spector (2017), Dr. Murray Grossan, an ENT otolaryngologist in Los Angeles, points to the science of psychoneuroimmunology (the study of how the brain is connected to the immune system), asserting that it has been shown "over and over again" that depression weakens your immune system, while happiness, on the other hand, has been shown to boost our body's immunity. "What's crazy is that just the physical act of smiling can make a difference in building your immunity," says Dr. Grossan. "When you smile, the brain sees the muscle [activity] and assumes that humor is happening."

LIFE COACH MOMENT

Tell yourself, "I WILL PROSPER IN ALL OF MY ENDEAVORS."
"I AM MAKING MORE EVERYDAY," "I HAVE LOVE AND RESPECT
FROM MY FAMILY," "MY ACTIONS CREATE SUCCESS."

Some of you may feel like these things are a waste of time; you may also feel like there is no way these things could possibly impact your life. I totally understand the challenges we all face as we make life changes, but do not despair. We must get uncomfortable in order for real change to take place. As you continue reading and visualizing these positive images, you will attract positive results. The results may be small, but know that they are a direct result of the aforementioned daily habit changes! That will be enough to keep you going; as you continue, more and more blessings and great things will come your way. Stay the course, believe in yourself, and know that you have what it takes to be better than you were yesterday. Fight for your future self!

3: CHANGING THE WAY YOU THINK ABOUT MONEY

It's time to get serious about this money discussion. I am going to make a statement that will probably shock most of my readers: *many people do not believe that they deserve an abundance of money*. There I said it! Sounds crazy, doesn't it? Well, many people talk about money, wealth, and things they would buy if they had money; however, the thought of seeing a large sum of money in their bank account is not realistic. What's even worse is that there are people who will actually show signs of resentment when they see others acquire an abundance of money. The truth of the matter is that money has carried a negative connotation for the masses of people. This is largely because (until recent years,) large sums of money appeared to be only available to the 'privileged' members of society. If you were extremely wealthy, you had to be either White or part of royalty.

The limited availability of large sums of money certainly does not apply today. People are making tons of money from building websites and apps from their bedroom while in pajamas. Others are becoming YouTube sensations or creating massive content on their favorite social media platform while cashing in on affiliate marketing. This is the greatest time in our history to make money with less resources. There is no need to doubt that prosperity and abundance can become your reality. Write down some goals, research, read, network with subject matter experts, and find a way to add value to something. The money will come; just don't ONLY focus on the money. Focus on doing something you love and adding value to the universe. Also, bury any negative feelings you have about money. Money serves a great purpose in society; you can be massively wealthy and still be a humble person who is of service to the world. You don't have to be an evil, arrogant asshole who drinks with their pinky sticking out. In fact, you do not have to show off your wealth. Live your life, set your goals, smash them, and grow your wealth without bragging. The hardest part of this entire journey will be convincing yourself that you are worthy of having a great life!

Your untrained mind will want to doubt you at every turn by telling you that your previous generations didn't have it, so it can't be possible for you. Your untrained mind may also tell you that because your uncle tried and failed at multiple business ventures, you will fail too. Nothing is further from the truth. People are different, as are circumstances, attitudes, and technology. So many things can alter your results, so how can you know what is possible? The attitude and determination that you use to approach matters is all that you can control.

Using money to impress others is another reason why many people are experiencing negative thoughts around money. Spending excessive money on material possessions, personal care (hair, face, etc.), or using your utility bill money to buy friends drinks at the club can leave you feeling disappointed after the money is gone. If you fall into these categories, don't feel bad. These are natural actions, especially since the visual media promotes a specific look to represent beauty. We must wear these clothes, drive that vehicle, or live in this neighborhood. Therefore, replacing these looks with images of what happiness and beauty looks like to me has become very important.

Obviously, as we get older and start maturing, we may do less to impress others, but not always. Sometimes, we go from trying to impress friends at school or college to trying to impress parents, family, and coworkers. This can be dangerous, especially if the desire to impress others comes at the cost of taking care of more important life matters. In many cases, you are working to impress someone who isn't even making your strides. Perhaps you have a friend or sibling you grew up with and competed with through the years; now that you both are adults, you find yourselves comparing spouses, jobs, income, children, or physical appearances. Doing this is a waste of time.

You should be supporting each other's advancements; you should also be helping your friend or sibling if you have reached a higher financial status than them. Money should be used to help people, not hurt them or tear them apart. Unfortunately, there are countless stories where money has been the instigator in horrible disputes; you can see why there is an unspoken negative aura related to having money. Again, resist these old ways of thinking. These are not real for your life. Separate yourself from any negative images of money. Think of the great things you can do for your immediate and extended family; think of the projects that you could invest in and the ways you can help your community or struggling friend find financial support for a business venture. Use money to have new experiences and see new places on this beautiful planet. Try not to be concerned with what others will think of you and, above all, stop holding onto negative thoughts about money. Those thoughts are the root of doubt that make you believe it to be true.

Since I grew up as a Black male in the East Bay area of California to a 'most-of-the-time' single mother, I am very familiar with getting by on a shoe-string budget. I am old enough to remember mom buying sneakers for me a couple times at a Safeway grocery store, believe it or not, or getting second-hand clothes at Goodwill. This may seem bad to some, but I didn't mind because I was always clean. The point is this: as a kid, funds were tight for me, and my mom and grandmother did their best to provide for me. My father was also supportive, but I was not living with him until I reached age 16.

When you grow up in predominantly Black neighborhoods, you get used to doing all that you can to save money or get something for the 'low-low.' It becomes part of your DNA, which is not all bad. Saving money helps if you can use it to become a prudent negotiator. The real issue is that when we are too tight on money, we send out an energy of lack or shortage, which is known as the scarcity mindset. The scarcity mindset occurs when you are afraid to spend money because you fear it will not circulate back to you; it is the belief that 'if I spend this money today, I will be broke tomorrow,' rather than thinking 'I will spend this money on the right things today, so that it comes back to me multiplied tomorrow.'

LIFE COACH MOMENT
Abandon the scarcity mindset and embrace the abundance mindset.

The scarcity mindset will block your pathway to prosperity. It causes you to restrict the passage for money to flow in. Unseen pressure causes everything to prevent you from releasing the money because your mind is telling you it will not return. Try to think of it in terms of playing basketball: if you are at the free throw line and fearful that you will not make that shot, there is a very high probability that you will not make that shot. However, if you approach each shot 'as if' you were confident that you will make it, you increase your odds of success. As you see one go in, and another go in, your confidence increases, and you start making them more frequently. The more that you *expect* money to come into your life, the more money *will* come into your life.

Like attracts like. Money attracts money. Spend money wisely and with good intentions, and the universe says, "Here is a person who appreciates the value of money; therefore, I must continue to provide more money for this person."

One way to begin to release the scarcity mindset is by finding ways to cut out the unnecessary spending in your life. This way, you will have more money for situations that money should be spent on. More money will give you more comfort.

Start focusing on eliminating money wasters, paying down debt and building an emergency fund. If you do nothing else after reading this book, please, at least, start paying closer attention to where your money is going. It has been said that, "Where a person spends their thoughts, they spend their money." Watch where your dollars are going and audit it monthly. Cut out things that are draining too much of your money. You will be surprised at how much money you will find that can be added back into your monthly budget.

Below are a few things that may immediately help you save a few dollars each month (thus adding money back into your budget):

- Unplug all cell phone chargers, when not in use. This means unplugging all electronics like toasters, coffee makers, and Alexa, when not in use. This goes for lights as well.

- Pack lunch at least two times per week instead of eating out. Cooking is beneficial and can become a soothing hobby.

- Make coffee at home instead of hitting Starbucks, Dunkin Donuts, or your favorite coffee shop.

- Use surge protectors to plug in TVs, game systems, and chargers. When you leave the house, turn off the surge protector (which disconnects all their energy sources at once) and then turn it back on when you get home.

- Drive more slowly. Driving over 60 miles per hour burns more gas. Also, remember to use the brakes less frequently. This is another gas drainer. Please adhere to all traffic regulations at all times.

- Use coupons and online discounts from your favorite grocery stores.

- Don't overdraw your bank account.

- Take a bike to work or school if at all feasible.

- Set a timer on your home thermostat.

- Learn how to cook.

- Adjust water heater temperature.

- Cut the cord; cut cable and get Netflix, Hulu, or Firestick.

- Read more often and watch less TV.

- Airbnb a spare bedroom.

- Rent out garage space.

- Rent your vehicle for magnetic signage.

- Stop one bad habit.

- Start a legal side hustle.

- Use Mint.com to track spending and create a budget.

- Take shorter showers.

- Work out at home instead of paying for a gym membership.

- Take better care of yourself to reduce healthcare expenses.

- Go to the movies during the day for matinee pricing.

- Drink more water.

- Carpool.

- Fill up your tires.

- Negotiate your utility bills.

- Start contributing to your 401k (and add 1% as often as possible; every quarter if you can afford it).

There are thousands of things that we can all do to eliminate money wasters in our lives. Dollars add up. Believe it or not, some of the aforementioned habits are necessary to become financially free. Financial freedom does not mean going out and buying the most expensive brand of items; it means that your expenses are managed by some forms of passive income, thus allowing you to discontinue working a traditional 9 to 5 job. The first step is reducing your expenses. Take action today to become financially free. You can do this.

FUN FACTS:

According to a Fidelity Net Benefits study,

A) The national average for 401k contributions is 5%. This means that of the Americans who have a 401k plan through their employer, the average percent of their paycheck being contributed to their 401k is 5%.

B) Forty-seven percent of the population has less than $1,000 saved for emergencies.

LIFE COACH MOMENT

True change is slow. Be patient. Focus on your results. Minor victories will be your saving grace.

4: MY TURNING POINT

Earlier, I mentioned that I have dreamt of being a millionaire since I was a child; those dreams and desires never really stopped. During my early and mid-20s, my determination to make big bonus checks and to become a manager was always there; it continued as I pursued some of my music business goals. At 27 years old, I, along with some other great guys (Charles 'SP' Honeycutt, Duane 'D'Webb' Webster, and Errol 'Reality' Kernihan), was an owner of a promotion company called Infinite Possibilities Open Mic Corporation. We promoted open mic events at the 'Historic' Royal Peacock Nightclub in Atlanta, Georgia; legends like Ray Charles, Aretha Franklin, and James Brown performed there in their heyday.

During this time, we were hitting the streets doing whatever we could to promote our event; mind you, this was just before the rash of social media sites started emerging. We used flyers, community radio, and word of mouth. Even though this was a modest form of promotion, we never had any doubt that this would lead to national acclaim as event promotors. As we hosted events, we met lots of talented entertainers in the Atlanta area.

Ultimately, I ended up managing one of the hottest, unsigned, female singing groups in the area known as Slick & Rose. As the manager of this dynamic duo, I experienced the true music industry life: touring, recording, marketing, scheduling, collecting per diems, selling merchandise, and selling an album called 'Objects in the Mirror.'

We toured The Blue Note Jazz Club in Nagoya and Osaka, Japan with Rich Nichols (manager of The Roots) and experienced fan followings. During this time in my life (2003), I had stopped working a 9 to 5 gig and became fully engulfed in the music and entertainment business. That meant that I had to make sure my hustle continued so the rent was paid, my three kids were still fed, and business expenses were covered. To do so, we were selling T-shirts, booking events, selling albums; however, independently of Slick & Rose, I was making a name for myself as an event host. I was emceeing every possible event that I could: poetry slams, hip-hop battles, comedy shows, community TV shows, and even a few concerts that came through town. As much as I loved living my dream as a professional music industry manager/host, I was not earning enough money to sustain.

In hindsight, there were some key decisions that may have advanced my music career, but my fear or doubt that it was possible for me to truly be wealthy caused my career to stall. During my late 20s and early 30s, I enjoyed a good five years or so of active involvement in the music business, but I did not achieve the financial freedom that I thought I was going to enjoy from that life. Moreover, that period did not help my credit score one bit. Remember, I traded in the office world of managing and making bonus checks for the glamour of being in the music business. That really set back my finances and I was also not as involved with my kids as I should have been. During this time, I also didn't have the best relationship with my children's mothers; this too had a negative impact on my life. How can I prosper if I am not actively involved in the lives of the children that I fathered?

This was my turning point. I knew I had to make better financial decisions and I had to do it immediately. In spring 2004, I decided to discontinue managing the singing group. At this point, I was doing very little hosting. It was back to what I knew best: collecting past due debts in collections. Having realized how difficult it was to manage my bills and lifestyle without a stable income, I decided to rededicate myself to moving up the corporate ladder. This time, I was in my early 30s and more mature; my time managing Slick & Rose added to my leadership skills. There was a renewed vigor in me and it drove me to be ultra-successful. I wanted to amass enough money to start living out my dreams. By this time my dreams were to get out of debt and earn over $100,000/year. I was also reading a lot of literature about successful people; I read books such as *The Autobiography of Quincy Jones, Think and Grow Rich: A Black Choice, The 7 Habits of Highly Effective People, Your Best Life Now*, and anything by Suze Orman. All of those books helped me get dialed in to where I wanted my finances and life to be.

LIFE COACH MOMENT

I also started receiving daily emails from THE SIMPLE DOLLAR. This is a daily email sent out that gives helpful advice on finances, saving, investing, getting out of debt, and overall financial literacy ideas.

I needed to be honest about all the obstacles in my path in order to confront them. It was time to take inventory of where I was with my debt and income; I also needed some kind of savings plan to build for my future. I can tell you that this was the most challenging part of my journey. Not only was it hard to compile all my debts and revisit the decisions that caused them but it also meant that I was officially going to have to change how I dealt with money; this was a pretty scary thought. My relationship with money would have to be viewed more as a business partner than an object.

I had to respect money differently and appreciate the things it could do in my life coupled with the lives of those that I am responsible for. This meant that I had to make new sacrifices and have the courage to turn down friends and family that wanted me to go places or do things with them. So, what did I do? I decided to take one bill at a time and contact the creditor (or collection agency). I was comfortable with this part since I, myself, was a debt collector and knew some of the strategies used to encourage people to pay their bills. Furthermore, I knew that I could increase my chances of getting them to accept a reduced pay-off (a settlement) to resolve the past due balance. I knew that whatever was negotiated needed to be supported with a written letter of agreement. (Just in case that employee left, I still had proof of the agreement.) I also knew that many of the collection agencies and collection law firms would be more willing to settle these debts during the last few days of the month. My focus was to stack as much money as I could by the month's end and contact as many of the creditors as I could to get them to accept lower pay-offs.

This strategy helped me clear up a few debts, but I wasn't bringing in enough money to settle out all the debt that I created. My next step was to closely review my credit reports to ensure the accuracy of the information. Of course, there were a couple of inaccurate reports or reports that were sold to debt buyers; therefore, I knew they may not have all the original documents. The most recent credit reporting laws require debt buyers and collection agencies to produce the original documents associated with a debt within 30 days of a dispute. Many agencies are not able to turn around the supporting information in the aforementioned amount of time. When that happens, the agencies have 30 days from that point to remove the debt from your credit report. Some agencies can compile the original documents fast enough, but they may have mix-ups or inaccuracies. If you opened a credit line before 2010 or so, the regulations were lighter for creditors as it related to consumer information gathering, excessive interest charges, and much more.

Before the Dodd–Frank Wall Street Reform and Consumer Protection Act was introduced into Congress, many creditors did not have solid processes regarding the storage of information; this resulted in files getting lost, merged, or destroyed. This is also one of the reasons why credit reporting agencies only give creditors 30 days to validate your debt or prove that you owe it (https://en.wikipedia.org/wiki/Dodd%E2%80%93Frank_Wall_S treet_Reform_and_Consumer_Protection_Act). This is a crucial step. It helped me greatly.

Let's re-cap a few key steps that I took that may help you with your credit score:

- Take inventory of all your debts, income and make a financial goal. I use www.CreditKarma.com to check my credit report. It is free and does not leave a hard credit inquiry on my credit score. I use www.Mint. com for tracking my income, spending, and setting financial goals. This, too, is free and does not hurt your credit score.

- Call creditors to negotiate reduced pay-off amounts (a.k.a. settlements). Some creditors will accept less than the full balance in exchange for a one-time payment to resolve the debt. This could be a great way to pay off more than one debt for the price of one. When negotiating these agreements, I suggest getting the terms outlined in writing BEFORE you make your payment. This will prevent future misunderstandings.

LIFE COACH MOMENT

It will take discipline to pay down your debt, but you can do this. Put something towards them every time you get paid, even if it is only $20

- Review your credit report(s) for inaccuracies and fraudulent claims. If you notice any information on your credit report that you believe to be incorrect (such as wrong balance dues, already paid off debts, balances that are not yours, etc.), you have the right to submit a dispute to the credit reporting agency. Send any supporting information that you have, and the agency will review over a specific amount of time (typically 30 – 45 days but could be extended). If they are unable to further support the claim, it must be removed or updated on your credit report. Eventually, this will come off of the report and your credit score may go up, depending on several factors. Visit https://www.ftc.gov/consumerprotection/credit-reporting for more information about Fair Credit Reporting.

Over the course of a couple years, I made some great strides to improve my credit. However, I was still well under a 650-credit score and failing to generate enough income to take care of all the debts on my report. I had to start making more money. To do that, I needed to get promoted at work and continue climbing up the corporate ladder. During this time, it was around 2005 or 2006. I was 31 or 32 years old and it was time to start making grown man money. My strategy became to build my 'personal brand' to reflect the level of knowledge and experience that I gained within the collections and customer service arenas. During this time, I was still managing and learning a lot about managing people. I realized that I was a good leader and many people were comfortable learning from me. This was great because I truly enjoy helping people.

I am an information junkie and love to share new information with as many people who will listen. When you begin to speak the life that you want for yourself, the universe will begin to mold the things around you into opportunities that could lead to the life you speak of. It was my desire to continue moving up the corporate ladder; not knowing how it would happen, I just continued to bring a positive attitude to work each day. I dressed like I was already at the next level, learned and researched as much about my job (and the next level job) as I could, and I thought positively. The more I learned, the more I was asked to train others. This led to a promotion, which gave me a 20% salary increase. I was happy. Then, the manager who promoted me was suddenly terminated; he ended up at another company and in a better position. Guess whom he called to come work with him? That's right... me! He set up a very informal interview with his boss and his boss's boss. I was hired on the spot; this doubled my most recent salary increase.

This experience taught me that I really could dictate the outcomes in my life. By bringing positive energy and specific thoughts to my mind and by truly believing in what I want, I can have anything that God desires me to have. There were some valuable lessons gained during the period in which I was receiving these promotions and increases; I also learned the power of setting goals, achieving goals through daily habits, being likable, and networking and building relationships. I will delve into these things more specifically in the next few chapters. I will end this section with the following tips for conquering your mindset!

PUTTING IT ALL TOGETHER – YOUR MIND IS READY!

- Be courageous.

- Be outstanding.

- Set goals.

- Smash your goals.

- Set more goals.

- Be thankful.

- Celebrate small victories.

- Know that YOU CAN DO THIS!

- Know that you have what it takes.

- Stay positive about everything.

- Expect a successful outcome in all ventures.

- Never apologize for being who you are.

- Be original.

- Be happy.

- Be creative.

- Be genuine.

- Help others.

- Exercise more often.

- Drink more water.

- Go to bed earlier; wake up earlier.

- Train your brain.

- Expect success.

SLICK & ROSE ALBUM COVER
Objects in the Mirror! (at Amazon.com)

SAMPLE VISION BOARDS

5: SETTING GOALS AND ACHIEVING GOALS

Most people realize that in order to achieve goals, there has to be a very specific image of the actual goal. Olympic sprinters can run extremely fast for 100, 200, and maybe even 400 meters, but there is no determined victor or completion of the race without an actual finish line. Goals require some basic image or picture of what success will look like once the goal is achieved. Therefore, the most important step when setting goals is: *creating the correct and most accurate image of victory for the goal to be achieved.*

If this is not done properly, you will be off track from the start. Quite often, I have told my son, "Start with the end in mind." This means start your journey with a vision of the journey's end as your first thought. If you were invited to a city over 250 miles from where you live, you would have to start with a thought of the city's location. This would determine the modes of transportation that you choose from, be it plane, train, or automobile. Your next thought might be how much money to set aside towards traveling. All your first decisions are based on the end destination; this same strategy should apply with your goals if they are to start off on the correct path.

Imagine that you have a daughter who comes home from school and informs you of her acceptance to a summer STEM program, one that she has wanted to attend for months. You are overjoyed and excited, until she says, "All you have to pay, Daddy, is $700 by the end of the month [which is in three weeks]." You will not let your daughter down, so you instantly establish a financial goal of $700 in 21 days. The $700 is the end goal; therefore, you are starting with 'the end in mind.' Next, you would research how much money you already have to put towards the $700. From there, your real grind kicks in; will your next check cover it? Will you need to work overtime? Is there another legal hustle you can do to get it? All of these thoughts come to mind.

Well, the first thing I would do is say to myself out loud, "I will get the $700 before the due date. I will get the $700 before the due date. I will get the $700 before the due date. I will get the $700 before the due date. I will get the $700 before due date." This is putting my mind on notice that we have a mission and we will accomplish it. We have a specific dollar amount and a specific date. In my heart of hearts, I will believe that it will happen. Remember, it is not my job to figure out all the steps that will make it happen; I just need to believe and take actions that are in my control.

Keep a positive attitude and reject any negative thoughts of doubt. Your brain will try to tell you that it will not work out because it didn't work out a previous time. When that pops in your head, immediately repeat the mantra.

This is how you take control of your thoughts. Within a week, you have secured $500 of the $700. Then, you check your mailbox and a $200 check from your Aunt Brenda is there. She attaches a card that reads, "I finally won at Bingo, thanks for the loan. Sorry it took so long to pay you back. Love You." You were not expecting that. In fact, you and Aunt Brenda got into it at Thanksgiving dinner last year because of this loan. The universe and God rewarded you for your trust and patience in positive energy. As I presented in that last scenario, you may have recalled a time when you had an unexpected stroke of luck or good fortune. You probably were in a good mood just prior to that. Do not underestimate the power of positive thoughts and speaking your reality into existence.

So, you now have a clear vision of what success looks like for your goal. *Write it down*. Whatever the goal is, please, write it down. Multiple times if you must. In fact, do it now. Get a piece of paper and write down a goal *right now*. You can write them on a goal board, which is similar to a vision board but without the pictures. Remember, start with the end in mind so that you have a clear vision of the goal. Set your goals with clear expectations in mind. No matter how lofty or big the goal is in your mind today, set it with the following attitude, "I will achieve this goal." Expect success. My goal board has exact dollar amounts (and other very specific items) that I am trying to achieve by a particular date with my net worth. Visualization will also help you see your goal come true.

Close your eyes and imagine that you are already celebrating the achievement of your goal. In this particular example, you would close your eyes and see yourself handing seven $100 bills to the coordinator of the summer STEM program for your daughter; you would visualize the smile on your face, the hand shake, maybe even the shirt you are wearing. Visualizing the exact moment of your goal's achievement has a power in and of itself. It makes the achievement possible. This is where the vision boards really have an impact; placing pictures of the goal on the board and seeing it each day will help attract the goal to you.

Visualization has helped me achieve so many of my goals. Seeing myself in my own office, on a cruise, or driving a specific vehicle has allowed me to live those moments out months later. It is truly fascinating. By visualizing your future, you are creating your future. Why wait for your boss or employer to dictate your future life? I promise you that their vision for you is not nearly as breathtaking as the one you imagine for yourself. Your boss or employer is up at night trying to find ways to get your job done for less money than they are paying you, while you are sitting back thinking you're in line for next month's pay increase.

You now have a clear goal because you started with the end in mind. You have written down your goal with an expectation of success. It is now time to speak your goal into reality. I know it probably sounds like hocus-pocus but stick with me for a moment. By speaking your goal out loud, it allows your goal to sink into your subconscious. Hearing the goal helps it manifest into your reality. Look at the goals that you have written down for yourself and read them out loud. Watch yourself say them as you look into your eyes in the mirror. Give them meaning and purpose; make them real via your conviction and passion. Increase the bass in your voice as you read these goals to yourself.

Throughout this book, I have stated this over and over: your subconscious mind will do whatever it is trained to do. You are training your brain to focus on your goal and the requirements to bring your goal into fruition. You can do this anytime and anywhere: in the car, in the shower, in the elevator while headed to your desk, anywhere! It is more than likely that you have already used this method to conquer a goal. Think of a time you may have told yourself, "I CAN DO THIS!" Maybe you were about to walk into an interview or give a speech. This is done to motivate yourself; this is a way to overcome the sticking points that we encounter when pursuing our goal. It is a way to stay focused on the mission at hand and press forward. The best time to recite your goals and positive affirmations is 10 to 15 minutes before you are going to sleep at night and then again during the very first moments that you wake up each morning. Continue to state them out loud every moment that you can without being disrespectful to others around you. People may begin to question your behavior, but most of those people are ones who don't believe you will get results from these actions. Let the naysayers have their negative thoughts; it should have nothing to do with you.

Speaking your goal into reality allows others to help you remain accountable for the goal. You may mention your goal to your spouse or a close friend; in turn, that person will ask you how things are progressing when they see you. This will put you in a state where you want to show progress has been made when you see them again. This person can also be known as your accountability partner. They can be another source of strength when you are having a rough time moving forward due to an unexpected obstacle.

Perhaps you mentioned to a friend that you have started taking cooking classes. If three months go by and you still do not know how to cook anything, it will be disappointing for both you and your friend. You spoke your cooking goal into the universe, yet you took no additional actions to make it a reality. Hope without work is useless. If we are to achieve our goals, it will require a combination of factors: determination, focus, positive thoughts, belief, speaking your goals out loud, reading them on your screensaver, dreaming about them, seeing them on your vision board or goal board, earning the support of others and the universe working in your favor.

LIFE COACH MOMENT

Be prepared for nonsupportive friends, family members, coworkers, neighbors, church members, and anyone else that notice your mindset changing. These are the reasons that people fail. They allow the negative thoughts of others (and themselves) to conquer their feelings of BELIEF! These same folks will say that they knew you could do it the whole time.

During the time I received promotions and salary increases, I was still determined to continue progressing. My children were teenagers and I was married with an additional daughter to help raise. My children and wife were a huge part of me achieving my goals. They were there for moral support on a daily basis; they were 'accountability partners' and my motivation to get my finances together. Sometimes, that's all a person needs to drive them to success. For me, it certainly helped.

By late 2009, I lost my good paying job due to a corporate shutdown. The worst part was that no severance pay was provided with my departure. I was temporarily devastated. My savings were not enough to make it for very long, so I immediately applied for unemployment and food stamps while I searched for a job. Fortunately, my name was good in the industry and many people assisted to help me find work. I landed a job at a small collection law firm. It paid some of the bills but only paid about 60% of my previous salary. Suffice it to say, the job was not working. I quickly fell back into debt, although not as bad as before, but it was a huge setback. This was another turning point for me! I began to focus on getting a better paying job. Here is where I started with the end in mind: based on my calculations, I needed to make at least $70,000/year to get out of debt, pay my current monthly bills for the house and family, and save enough money to get married and buy a house. My plan was to get all of this within a year and the date was 9/1/2010. What did I do? I created a goal sheet with these things on it! It looked something like this one below:

VIC'S GOAL SHEET (AS OF 9/1/2010)
- Find a job earning at least $70,000/year (preferably with bonus opportunities) by 1/1/2011.

- Pay off student loans of $2,500 by 3/31/2011.

- Get married by fall 2011.

- Pay off loans and credit cards by 6/1/2011.

- Get credit score to 650 by 9/1/2011.

- Save $10,000 for down payment on a house by 9/1/2011.

- Maintain perfect health.

Accomplishing each one of these goals *before* the deadline date that I entered on the goal board became my objective. Each morning, I started repeating the goals out loud as I prepared for work; I repeated them again in the evening when I was winding down. My mind began to focus on things that would draw these results closer to me; suddenly, I would see books related to interviewing, or literature and Internet sites that covered ways to reduce my monthly expenses. As I learned something that I felt would help me achieve one of the goals, I implemented it into my daily habits. All the while, Latasha and I were discussing areas in town that we really wanted to move to; this was before we were financially ready. It was important to me to get her excited about our future, so she would keep me motivated when I was running low on drive.

Within a few weeks of me writing down the aforementioned goals, I received an email from a former colleague who went through the corporate shutdown. He was doing recruiting and came across a position that he felt I would be great for. I met with him for lunch (my treat, since he was helping me) and he told me everything I needed to know about the company, their future, their management team, and what they were looking for in the role. It was beyond my previous experience, but close enough that I was confident that I could GROW INTO THE POSITION. My colleague felt the same way. He helped me reorganize my resumé and update my LinkedIn profile and gave me some great interview advice.

I got the first interview, then the second interview, and then I got silence for a few weeks. By now, it was early December 2010 and I was still struggling with the monthly bills. I recall speaking to my dad at the time (who is usually very supportive) about how I'd been waiting awhile with no update. My dad made a statement that I will never forget. He said, "Good luck getting the job, Son, but don't be surprised if they overlook you for someone with a college degree." My response to him was, "I may not have a college degree, but I am definitely the most qualified for this job." I'm sure he was not trying to be mean, but it upset me that my dad doubted me. There was no doubt in my mind that I was going to get that job. I continued reading my goal board and praying that I get an update on the job.

On New Year's Eve (12/31/2010), Latasha and I were home alone, and I said, "We should go ahead and get married at the court house, so we can start 2011 off blessed." She agreed. We joined our church on Sunday (1/1/2011). Monday (1/2/2011) was a holiday, so we were married on Tuesday, (1/3/2011). One goal was accomplished early! On 1/11/2011, I received the call I'd been waiting for, "Victor Johnson, this is Robert with Title Masters. I would like to offer you the servicing manager role with a starting salary of $72,000/year plus monthly bonus opportunities." I accepted the job and two goals were accomplished!

As each goal was checked off the list, my confidence went higher and higher. That's the momentum you get from success. The energy of accomplishment fills you, your perception gets clearer, you have bounce in your walk, and you smile and speak with vigor. These feelings will multiply. There is a compound effect happening from the accomplishment of your goals. I was literally speaking my goals into reality. The daily habits of speaking the goals, seeing the goals, thinking the goals, and breathing the goals were bringing them to my front door. This process became habitual after a while and it was exciting to put those slashes through the paper on my mirror.

A few months into the Title Masters gig, I was bringing in nice bonus checks and using them to pay down debts and save money whenever I could. However, there was one particular 'splurge' when I got my first bonus check, which was probably $2,500 on top of the regular check. I took my kids to Tanger Outlet Mall and gave each one $100 before we got out of the car. Part of this was an exercise to learn about my kids' money habits, but mainly, I wanted to reward them for their support during the lean months. The youngest (14) was broke in 30 minutes, the next youngest (15) spent about $25, the two older ones (20 & 17) got something to eat and pocketed about $90 each. It was a fun day for us all.

Latasha and I were able to strengthen our income and credit scores enough to start talking about actually buying a home for the first time. We also knew that we needed to get preapproved for a home loan. I still had a few tax liens hindering my credit from earlier business ventures and it was negatively impacting our ability to get preapproved. Therefore, it was time for me to put my pride aside and allow Latasha to seek preapproval without me. This was tough for me since I was basically agreeing to let her put the home in her name without my name. Since age 17, my name was on the lease of any place I considered my residence; at that time, in my limited mind, not having my name on the loan made me feel like 'less of a man.'

Once we got passed that, she applied for a home loan and was preapproved for $80,000; we were very excited. We immediately started looking for homes that were in that price range and close to our kids' schools and our family. We found the perfect little 3-bedroom, 2-bathroom, 1-car garage home, with a beautiful backyard view of Stone Mountain. This was the same Stone Mountain that the good, Reverend, Dr. Martin Luther King, Jr. mentioned in his 'I Have A Dream' speech: "Let freedom ring from Stone Mountain of Georgia... every hill and mole hill of Mississippi..." Okay, I digress.

At the time, the house was the right size for our family and convenient for all the things going on in our lives. The best part is that the purchase price of that home was $51,000, which would later prove to be a great thing. Now we just had to keep saving money and continue working on our credit scores, particularly mine. Ultimately, with a little down payment assistance from my grandmother, we were able to close on this beautiful home on 8/20/2011. Three goals were accomplished, and a fourth goal was accomplished because I was able to maintain perfect health. I did all this in under one year! It is possible to accomplish your goals on your terms within your timelines! The goals that I accomplished that year were because of my complete devotion to my daily habits: reading; speaking my goals out loud; praying; thinking positively; expecting my goals to be accomplished; acting 'as if' I were already living out the results of my goals; exercising regularly; getting support from my kids, wife, friends, and family; and believing in myself!

"Act as if. Act as if you're a wealthy man, rich already, and then you'll surely become rich. Act as if you have unmatched confidence and then people will surely have confidence in you. Act as if you have unmatched experience and then people will follow your advice. And act as if you are already a tremendous success, and as sure as I stand here today – you will become successful." —Jordan Belfort, *The Wolf of Wall Street.*

"When facing a difficult task, act as though it is impossible to fail. If you are going after Moby Dick, take along the tartar sauce." —H. Jackson Brown, Jr.

Acting 'as if' is imitating a behavior or a person. If you have a positive role model who is successful in a career that you are pursuing, you would research as much as you could about how that person got to where they are today. You would research the career in depth, interview subject matter experts, and maybe even dress like them. If we would 'act as if' we were already doing the things that we wish we were doing, we would find more success. 'Act as if' we were already in our desired work position, or 'act as if' we had already lost those 25 pounds, or 'act as if' we were debt-free, we will eventually experience these things in the flesh. Acting 'as if' we were already living the life we desire is one of the key strategies to accomplishing our goals.

An internship is another example of a modeling individual. Anyone who is part of a network that teaches them a particular skillset (such as a real estate investing network or sales network) is modeling the instructors as they have already assumedly excelled in the craft. If they have proven to be successful in their craft or skill, why deviate? At the very least, don't deviate until you have excelled and would want to continue to innovate in that particular skill.

Throughout my many and varied careers, I have found at least two people whom I could model (whether known or unknown to me). This encouraged me to reach new heights, since I'd already read about or observed someone else doing it at a high level. When I was 20 in 1994, Puffy Daddy (now known as Diddy) was really taking off with his entertainment company, Bad Boy

Entertainment. He was a student at Howard University just a few years prior. During my junior year in high school, I attended a college tour in Washington DC; we visited several HBCUs (Historically Black Colleges and Universities); Morgan State (Baltimore), Norfolk University, and Howard University. I was amped about Howard; I applied my senior year and was accepted.

Well, by the start of my senior year, I suddenly had to move from Richmond, California to Decatur, Georgia to live with my dad, stepmother, and two sisters. That changed my financial aid situation since my dad and stepmom were higher earners than my mom at that time. Financial aid was denied, and I was stubborn about taking a student loan; therefore, there was no Howard for me. I have no regrets about it at all. I avoided thousands of dollars of student loan debt and still ended up excelling in life (at a fairly young age to boot).

In 1994, I was just getting into the music phase of my life (promoting and rapping). Puff Daddy was doing some really creative forms of marketing and promotions; I was fascinated, especially since he was not much older than I was. I modeled many of his promotional tactics with my local events and also started managing artists around that time. This led me to a nice run of promoting and management of artists, including my stint with Slick & Rose, which led us to Japan on the Black Lily Tour through the Blue Note Jazz Cafés. Those are experiences that will live with me forever; I'm sure my kids are worn out from my 'throwback' stories and pictures. Modeling Puff helped me achieve these things, and I didn't even realize that's what I was doing.

LIFE COACH MOMENT

Work on your goals no matter how long they take; the years will continue to go by anyway. Four years is four years whether you are doing something or not.

All successful people have, and may still, model someone whom they admire in their craft (unless they are at the top of their craft). If they're at the top of their craft, then they are being modeled! At the time when my wife and I purchased our home and I was earning a better salary, I was still encouraged to push further. My debts were not yet completely cleared out (but I did pay my grandmother back). My kids were getting closer to graduation and I had very little money saved (which, for a mid-30s guy, isn't good). I began to visualize myself as a successful businessman, with all of the so-called successful businessman accessories (laptop, executive attire, office, traveling for business, and so on). I began to model businessmen whom I saw coming to meet with my bosses. I also modeled professionals whom I ran into at the weekly auto auctions for our company. I even modeled business professionals whom I saw in the *Fortune Magazines* that came to my home each month for years. I was reading them as a bachelor in my early 20s. I always had my mind on my money and money on my mind.

As the months went by, my teams continued to perform well, and I was able to continue advancing others around me; this is key. Helping others must be part of your mindset in all of your endeavors or you will run into obstacles at every turn.

I carried myself like an executive each day; I wore ties to work when others wore jeans. I researched all I could about the collection and auto recovery industry (repossessing cars and selling them at auctions). It was a tough job, but someone had to do it. It was so important to me that I continued to build a solid network of associates that I could reach out to if I needed a positive reference (or if I could assist them in any way). These actions were pushing me to new career levels that I had not previously experienced, and I was proud of the progress that was being made. Of course, I used the advancement to pay down my debts, start saving more money, work on our new home, support the teens with all their life activities, start taking annual summer family vacations, and still plan for the future. Acting 'as if' and modeling behavior patterns worked for me. If you are pursuing a specific path, find that perfect person to model and 'act as if' you were already winning!

I must say, I am truly blessed and thankful to God, as I know that HE has been my strength my entire life. I am writing this book and telling you of the actions that we can take as human beings to HELP create wealth and happiness for our lives and our families, but none of it is possible without God. I am truly, truly thankful. Glory to God!

Let's recap my keys to setting and accomplishing goals. Be sure to attack them with energy, enthusiasm, and passion!

- Start with the end in mind (a.k.a. have a clear vision of what the goal is).

- Write down your goal (preferably multiple times).

- Set the goal with the attitude of success (a.k.a. expect success).

- Speak your goals into reality. (This will help motivate you.)

- Act 'as if' the goal were already accomplished. (Model someone who is already successfully doing what you are striving to do.)

6: LET'S TALK ABOUT HEALTH & DAILY HABIT CHANGES

My physical health is the most important thing to me. I realize that without good health, everything in my life will be much more challenging. Since I was a preteen, I have taken great pride in my physical health. My father has always been a physically built guy throughout his life; however, he was short in comparison to most men. My mother has always been slim and taller in comparison. Somehow, I ended up being short and slim (which I love, now that I am in my mid-40s).

Both of my parents have always been very physically active and conscious of their eating habits. Those same attributes carried over to me. I was also raised by my grandmother, who was a nurse for over 25 years. She was always very aware of germs and wanted all her children and grandchildren to be clean. Her eating habits were also healthy throughout her older years. These three individuals shaped my mentality about taking care of my physical self, but I also had a few buddies who were serious about working out and taking care of their bodies.

My friend D'Webb is about 14 years older than I am. When he was 32 and I was 18, we started exercising after work. He taught me lots of smart muscle shaping exercises as well as the importance of maintaining a strong core (stomach, back, and chest areas). These places are where your balance is maintained. To this day, he is pushing 60 and is one of the most fit guys you will see in that age group. Also, my close friend S.P. has always been into working out and building muscle. S.P. was more of a cerebral fitness guy; he knows what each muscle in your body should do, what impacts them, how to grow them, etc. He keeps a nice amount of weights and work out gear available; I have worked out with him quite a bit through the years. I and these guys have spent the past 25 years (30+ for D'Webb) working on our physical health.

At the time this was written I was 44 and I couldn't be more thankful that my health was always at the forefront of my mind. I am the guy who turns anything into a workout. There were times when I was single, my buddies would come over to hang out and while we were all talking, I would break out into a set of 20 push-ups or start doing lunges. When I was cooking, I would start doing push-ups against the kitchen counter or walk up and down the stairs in my living room a few times to get my body moving. It has been said that, "A body in motion, stays in motion." So, stay moving!

Do not underestimate the value of stretching your body. Stretching will help you to maintain your elasticity (a.k.a. flexibility). We feel so much better when our muscles are loose. Stretching just before you go to sleep, and when you first get up in the morning, is essential to good health. You are probably realizing that I have some habitual rituals that I perform before and after sleeping. Reading my goals and positive affirmations and stretching during these times are important to the continual development of my mind, body, and soul. Many people have told me that I "have the mind of a man 10 years older than me, but the physical health and appearance of a man 10 years younger than me." What a great compliment is that? Imagine being more mature mentally, yet youthful in appearance and health.

Taking care of your health has tremendous financial benefits as well. Think of all the prescription medications that some of your friends or family members may be taking; maybe you are on some prescribed medications. You may be able to reduce the need for these pharmaceuticals. Your body is built and created to heal itself if you are taking care of it properly. There is a saying, "the doctor dresses the wound, but the body heals it." As a child, I was very active and nearly every weekend I would cut my skin open from falling or playing too aggressively. I would run home crying and mom (or grandma) would put some painful alcohol or peroxide on my skin to kill the bacteria, and they would wrap it. Within a day or so, I would remove the wrap or Band-Aid and within a couple more days, there was little to no sign that I cut that skin open. My skin healed the wound itself; our entire body operates like this. Unfortunately, through the centuries, our habits and lifestyles have eroded some of the healing effects that the body needs.

Below are some daily habits you can try that will promote better health:

- Drink water and green tea.
- Stop drinking sugary drinks and soda!

- Do push-ups.
- Do squats.
- Walk up and down the stairs at work and at home more often.
- Eat more fruit.
- Go for a walk outdoors.
- Inhale fresh air.
- Read about healthy things for your body and mind.
- Make your lunch.
- Go without the salt!
- Go without the sugar!
- Stop smoking cigarettes.
- Get a physical and regular health screenings.
- Get your teeth cleaned and checked annually.
- Find ways to move your body more often. (Do pushups against the kitchen counter, etc.)
- Sweep, vacuum and mop the floors in your home. (This is exercise too.)
- Check YouTube for quick in-home workouts that you can do – no gym membership required. And if you have a gym membership, USE IT at least two times per week.
- Get no less than seven hours sleep each night. Play basketball, jog, Zumba, dance. (Do anything to get your heart beating faster for an extended period of time.)

Obviously, we all are different people, so we will have very different daily habits. Based on where you live, where you grew up, what your culture is, how many people rely on you each day, and many other things, we will have varying degrees of busyness. No matter what your routine is, there are some key things that successful people add to their daily habits to ensure a continued pattern of success within their endeavors. Here are just a few of those daily habits:

- Wake up early.

- Pray (or meditate based on their spirituality).

- Read daily (particularly books).

- Exercise or stretch.

- Have a balanced diet.

- Find ways to develop themselves daily.

- Manage expenses.

- Write down goals.

- Drink more water (or Green Tea).

- Make their beds (this is a symbol of organization and cleanliness).

- Consult their mentor/spend time with their mentee.

- Spend time with their family (in home companions).

Over the past five years, I have worked all of these practices into my daily habits. Of course, there will be days when I don't get to all of them, for any number of reasons, but, in general, I make sure they're accomplished on a daily basis. These habits become patterns that help me to conquer any obstacles that may challenge my destiny. There is another benefit for me; if I achieve each of these daily habits by the end of the day, I feel victorious and satisfied. This allows me to have daily success stories. With each daily victory, my confidence grows. With increased confidence, my positive energy also increases. With more positive energy, I attract more positive events and experiences. This all leads to continuous success. There is no secret to success. It really is that simple. Successful people from all walks of life will share similar stories, with their own twists. It all boils down to doing the right things every day to improve yourself. The hard part is, doing the right things every day to improve yourself. Get it?

We are usually our biggest obstacle to achieving the wealth and happiness that we seek. The good news is: now that you know, you can make the change beginning now. If you really want this great life of wealth and happiness, don't just talk about it; be about it! Take a leap of faith on yourself. What do you have to lose? If you are not happy with the life that you are currently living, stand up and take action *now*! It really is that simple. It is not a matter of waiting for the 'just right moment' because things never seem to be absolutely perfect for us to make a change. It is usually the excuses, "as soon as I get this bill paid off, I'll go back to school," "as soon as the summer is over, I'll start my exercise plan," "as soon as my taxes come back, I'll start a business." The truth is, *now* is as good a time as ever. We are not promised tomorrow, and days turn into years faster than we realize. The worse that could happen is that you may fail... and so what? Learn from it, dust yourself off, try again. Fail differently if you have to. Learn, try again, and succeed!

Here's another thing: get away from toxic people. These are people who always have bad news or gossip to spread; they want to dog out your plans and ideas. Get them away from you as fast as your body can move. Block them from all of your social media if you have to. During the initial phases of making a positive and dramatic change in your life, you cannot allow any negative thoughts to infiltrate your mind. These folks have nothing good up their sleeves and are probably disappointed that they have not started on that lifelong idea that they had. I call them 'doppelgangers.' Doppelgangers are ghostly doubles of a person who suck or drain the energy or soul from your body (at least that is my definition of doppelganger). If you are the one getting in your own way, change that. The only limitations are the ones that we set on ourselves. Be relentless and fearless; you have no clue what the outcome will be. If you're like me, you will see no other result, except the winning result.

The point is this: stay the course and remain focused on what you need to do. Do not get sidetracked with the bullshit. Be strong, be determined. We are in a world full of information and resources these days; if you need something, Google it. I realize that there are some people reading this book who are in horrible relationships, particularly in which the other person is abusive (verbally, physically, or spiritually). Get the help that you need; get out of that environment. Go to a church, friend, family member, or any other safe place and build from there. *Do not let someone take you away from the life that you deserve.*

Yes, it will be hard in the beginning, but your hard work and belief will be rewarded. Don't give up on this process. It will take days, weeks, months, and years to truly achieve your goals and, even then, you should not stop going after bigger goals! I always tell myself, my kids and wife, and anyone else who will listen to "plan the work and work the plan." (This is a quote from the great, Napoleon Hill, Author of *Think and Grow Rich*.) Plan your moves and take action.

LIFE COACH MOMENT

Find someone to help today. It can be the smallest thing: give someone a snack, smile, say hello, let someone use your cell phone charger. It can be small but do it. Helping someone else will release positive energy through your body, which will help you conquer the day.

7: BEING LIKEABLE/NETWORKING/ RELATIONSHIP BUILDING

Along my journey, I must admit that there has been one asset that has afforded me great opportunities and experiences; that is my SMILE! I have always been a smiling face as a baby, kid, teen, and as a young and middle-aged man. It is just me. Whether you call me Jabo, Nico Don, Don, Victor, Mr. Johnson, or Vic, you usually see my smile before you see anything else on me. It is genuine, too! I am generally a happy person with a positive outlook on life, and that was before I was as successful as I am today. Both my mother and my father are humorous, witty, and outgoing; I must have inherited those great qualities from them (my kids inherited those smiles as well). For me, I am smiling most of the time because I am happy with what I have accomplished in my life. At each level, I have reflected on my journey and the struggles, and it gives me an appreciation for what I have. Of course, I am always striving higher so that I can build on the legacy that my grandmother left behind, but I am ever so grateful for the life that I live. I love my life.

It is important to carry a smile when you meet people; it lets them know that you are open to meeting them. Perhaps there has been a time when you hung out with a friend and they brought along a new person to the group who may not have had a good vibe or good energy. More than likely, that impression was developed because the person was not smiling during the very first interaction.

Obviously, I have not been privy to sit in on the hiring meetings after my interviews, but I would suspect that two things came up, 1) "He had a great smile," and 2) "He presents well (or he was well dressed)." I am not boasting when I tell you these things; they were deliberate actions of mine to help swing interviews in my favor. When you are seeking a job, I would hope that you do all that you could to present your best self. It doesn't require lots of money, either. I have purchased nice dress slacks, shirts, and blazers from Goodwill and thrift stores. I washed them and had no shame about it. My father has given me work attire, such as ties and cuff links, and I have done the same for my son. Start where you are and build from there but know that *it takes no money to smile.*

Now I will say that it helps to keep your teeth as healthy and as clean as possible. I admit that due to the volume of tea I've consumed through my life, my teeth are not the whitest. However, they are straight, and I take proper care of them. Why do I do these things? I do these things because I would like to present a 'likable' personality.

Being likable will open doors that some advanced skills will not open for you. Having the ability to attract people with your pleasing personality shows that you can deal with other people. If you were super talented in a specific skill but had a shitty attitude all the time, hiring managers will pass on you and take the less skilled candidate with the great personality. They could always train the skill, but it is difficult to train a person to change their personality. Think about the people in your work place and schools; you may have instantly thought of that one person who always has a bad attitude, no matter what is going on. How could that person continue to advance in their career if they were to continue to carry themselves in that manner? They probably would not get very far. Worse yet, are YOU that person in your office? If you are, it may be difficult to confront that reality, but that is part of this process. Please be mature and determined enough to accept that your attitude may be the one that requires adjusting.

For many of us, there are things far back in our past that may place a semipermanent hardened look on our face; it has been there so long, that we have gotten used to it. Once this is realized, it can be altered. If it is an issue for you, it's important to take this step. It will be difficult to meet new people who can assist along your path. Word has always traveled fast, but never faster than it does today. If you have offended someone in business, it will travel to thousands of people before you have left the room. One of those thousands, if not hundreds of thousands, could be a client whom you need for your business, or a potential business partner of your desire. Once the word is out, it could, at the very least, slow down your progress while questions are being asked about your character.

Being likable also will serve you well as you begin to network with others who can assist you on your path to wealth and happiness. Hands down, networking is the single most important step in becoming successful. We can do a lot of things in life, but not many things can be done well on our own. People make the world go around; therefore, we must interact with people to reach our goals. Per Dictionary.com:

Networking (noun)

>A supportive system of sharing information and services among individuals and groups having a common interest

As a verb (used without object):

>To cultivate people who can be helpful to one professionally, especially in finding employment or moving to a higher position

No matter the career path that you are venturing into, you will want to network with others who are serious about the craft. Networking allows us to add information to a group of like-minded individuals, while also learning from the group. Collaborative thinking advances our life's best work. Through your network, you can meet others who have similar interests and may have a need for your services or products. Networking also allows us to strengthen the string of people that we know in life. One thing that life has taught me is that you usually run into people at least twice in your lifetime. Sometimes you need them for a purpose or they need you for a purpose; nevertheless, it definitely helps to have had a positive experience with them during previous interactions.

My last three jobs were a direct result of networking. Back in the summer of 2013, I was working for a company called Title Masters in John's Creek, Georgia. The company made plans to shut down within the next 12 to 18 months, so they were slowly releasing staff and paying them severance packages based on their tenures and job functions. Being the servicing manager, I was asked to stick around to help dissolve the business and potentially sell off the remaining portfolio of business. As part of my duties during this phase, I was asked to follow up with a few potential buyers to gauge their interests. In one of those conversations, I spoke to a young woman who worked for a competitor (EZCORP), named Natalie Varner (now Lampis). Little did I realize that the conversation would have a positive impact on three major future events in my life. After speaking to Natalie for an hour about the industry, staff, processes, procedures, and our business, she said she would contact me in a couple days with a final decision about purchasing the portfolio. Two days later, she called me and said, "Hey Vic, we decided to pass on the portfolio; however, reach out to me when you are done with your duties at Title Masters. I have an opportunity for you." Obviously, I followed up with her. She set up an interview for me with her company for a role that would have placed me over seven stores in the Atlanta market. I was excited, even though this was beyond my scope of talents. I'd never remotely managed several teams before. Well, due to the extensive Call Center Management experience on my resume, I was presented with a more lucrative opportunity of managing the National Call Center in Austin, Texas; relocating was not on my family's radar, especially since we had only been in our home for two years.

They flew me out to visit the EZCORP Austin Corporate offices and I was hooked. I got an offer that would pay me a base, annual salary of $100,000, plus quarterly bonuses, a relocation package to move to Texas, and great benefits. Now, all I had to do was convince my wife and kids that this was the right move due to the tremendous financial increase it would provide for us. One of my daughters (Jasmine) and my son, (Jahree), ended up staying in Georgia since they were so close to graduating from high school. Their mother and grandparents took them in. My wife and stepdaughter (Tai), were the only ones left to convince. Latasha and Tai stayed in Georgia while we found a buyer for the house. Meanwhile, I headed to Austin to get to work and start setting up a new life for us. More on this transition will come a little later.

The next time networking helped me get a job was two years later in 2015. In July 2015, my boss at EZCORP informed me that the company decided to shut down one half of the business (the loan side of the business, which was the side that I worked for). She was completely distraught to tell me this since she'd hired me and convinced me to relocate my family to Austin, Texas. Her name was Leigh Ann Lindsey (to this day, she is a true friend of mine). This shutdown was inevitable; yet again, I was asked to stick around to help dissolve the business. This, too, came with a lucrative severance package if I stayed until the end (which was another four months). During that time, I decided to inform my LinkedIn network that I would be available for new opportunities by the beginning of December 2015. Those four months were awesome for me, because they allowed me to start working on my real estate investing business.

A few weeks after I sent out the message to my LinkedIn network, I heard back from a colleague named Debra Tucker. Back in 2009, I was working for the collection law firm that shut down, Mann Bracken. Before leaving, I made sure that I added as many of those talented people to my network as possible; that proved to be a great decision. Debra called me and told me about a colleague she knew in Austin who needed someone with my skillset to help build the compliance team for a debt buyer. Through Debra, I met Ken Luster and interviewed with him. The best part about this opportunity is that it was literally three blocks away from my EZCORP office. The timing was perfect; I ended my duties at EZCORP on 11/30/2015 (and got my $30,000 severance check) and started working with Ken Luster on 12/15/15. There was a slight decline in pay, but the convenience of the location made up for the pay decrease.

The point is this: here are two individual situations in which networking had a direct impact on the advancement of my career. These were not $1.00 or $2.00/hr. increases; the EZCORP move was a $40,000/year increase in my salary. The move to work with Ken Luster did not give me a salary increase, but it was a smooth transition to a good job as I continued to develop myself and work on my real estate investing education.

The third job I got through networking came during the summer of 2017. I was content working with Ken Luster and growing my real estate portfolio when I received a call in January 2017 from an old friend, Natalie. Before I tell you what happened on that call, I must tell you how Natalie assisted my family a second time after helping me get the job at EZCORP. In early 2016, Natalie was no longer working at EZCORP and she decided to get her real estate license. It just so happened that Natalie ended up being our realtor for the first primary home that we bought in Texas. What an angel! So, first she played a major role in getting me hired with EZCORP, which tremendously increased my income; then, she was our superb realtor who helped us buy the home of my family's dreams.

By January 2017, Natalie had stopped doing real estate and gotten back into the financial services business (with a very large player in the industry). Natalie called me to see if I was interested in an opportunity with the company, but I would have to relocate to Dallas, Texas (which was four hours from the Austin area). Initially, I told her that I was fine where I was, especially since my family and I hadn't been in our new home a full year yet. A couple months passed by and I decided to text Natalie just to see if she ever filled the role. She said 'no.' I told her to throw my name in the hat and see what happens. In this situation, I was not pressed to move or leave my current job, but I was always intrigued with advancing myself. With the opportunity, I could be more in control of the terms of the agreement, especially since I did not have to move or take the job. They made an offer that was very lucrative and inclusive of relocation costs. By this time, my kids had graduated high school and were attending college. I looked at this as an opportunity to grow our real estate portfolio; we could maintain the rental that we purchased in 2015 (details will be discussed in the next two chapters); we could rent out our home (that would be tough to convince Latasha) and purchase property in the Dallas area that could be rented out at a later date. I accepted the job and started in June 2017.

Without networking, none of these opportunities would have come my way. Moreover, being likable, staying positive, and focusing on the things that I wanted for my life drew opportunities closer to me. Working hard and being a good person who always tried to help people at work, caused me to stand out. Though it was unfortunate to know that I was losing my job, I was happy to stay and make more money until the end. There is no way that I could have predicted or planned these events, especially in the order of occurrences; but, my mindset was locked into the success and goals that I wanted for myself and my family. Therefore, God and the universe saw to it that these events came to fruition.

Here are some tips that may help you become more likable and build your network.

- Smile often.

- Be grateful for what you have in this moment.

- Create a www.LinkedIn.com profile. (This should only be for your professional networking; this should not be used like Facebook or Instagram.)

- Periodically reach out to people to check on them.

- Go to networking events in your local area.

- Join www.MeetUp.com (to meet local groups of people with a number of interests from cooking to real estate investing to marathon running).

- Go golfing (at local courses for a much lower cost).

- Attend charity events.

- Register for free seminars and educational events at libraries and community colleges.

- Go to bookstores.

- Visit art galleries.

- Go to a Toastmaster (https://www.toastmasters.org/) event to better your public speaking skills.

- Negotiate from a win-win mentality (where both parties should feel as though they got something out of the deal).

- Publicly praise people. ("Great job with that assignment earlier," "You always have a great attitude.")

- Say "thank you" as often as possible.

- Be humble.

- Look people in the eye.

- Stand up when shaking someone's hand (if you are seated).

- Compliment people on things (such as what they have on, their smile, their comments).

- Stop complaining. (No one really cares!)

- Call people by their names. (People love hearing their name.)

- Call people on the phone sometimes.

- Help others.

- Give without expectations.

- Laugh a lot!

- Say positive things about people.

- Stop gossiping.

- Refer people to others so they can help each other.

In my career and life, I have made many mistakes. Some had significant impacts and others were less impactful but provided me with a lasting lesson. In my younger days, (we're talking late teens and 20s), my first reaction was to immediately identify who caused it and why (and to place blame elsewhere), but as I have transitioned into my mid-life, my first reaction is to look at what I may have done. The younger me is very similar to the masses of people who say, "Whose fault is this" with fingers pointed. However, that reaction only creates animosity, anger, retaliation, and so on.

I started to consider the alternative. I took a quick analysis to see if there was anything that I could have done differently on my end. "Did I explain myself clearly?" "Did I send a mixed message?" "Was I being selfish?"

All these questions show that you are thinking of the other person. Before you approach them with an accusatory tone, take a quick assessment of what you could have controlled. Even if you believe you've done nothing, the other person may have an entirely different perspective about the situation. It's always better to take the high road and say something like, "It appears that I may have said something that has offended you and that certainly was not my intent. If so, I do apologize." Yep, I'm actually suggesting an apology (sometimes), especially if you've knowingly offended someone else. It comes down to the golden rule: "Do unto others as you would want done unto you."

During my management career, there were plenty of moments when I made mistakes, especially as I was promoted into new roles. I made errors on reports and during presentations in front of key executives, I've sent out emails to my teams with mistakes in them, and so on.

Each moment presented its own embarrassment and disappointment and even a few reprimands. Those mistakes were hard to swallow and definitely hard to bounce back from.

A few years back in 2010, when I ended up working at a collection law firm in Roswell, Georgia, I was in the role as the general manager of a call center. This was an extremely small company with maybe 15 total employees in the Roswell location and another 20 or so in a Kentucky office. My team had only four employees (including me) since this was a new strategy to have collection staff in the Roswell office. (I was hired to get it up and running.)

Eventually, we began to have weekly or bi-weekly conference call meetings with the Kentucky office; we would discuss numbers and strategies, etc. Each department head would run through their information and answer any questions from the boss. During one particular meeting, I botched the numbers and it caused much confusion on the call. The boss was livid and did not hold back his feelings about it. As I tried to clean things up, it only made matters worse.

This was the first time I'd made such a huge mistake in front of such an audience. What made it worse was that I could not respond in my usual manner since I was among a different audience. The rest of the week was horrific for me. I did not walk through the office with the same swagger; I spoke with less bravado and I avoided my boss as much as possible.

Keep in mind that this was a few months after I was released from Mann Bracken due to corporate shutdown. I accepted this job to pay the bills, but I was making much less than before, and my bills were quickly falling behind. This was having a terrible impact on my relationship with my wife due to the level of stress I was carrying. My confidence was at its lowest. The weekend had finally arrived, and it could not have showed up fast enough; that evening, I smoked weed until I passed out!

The next morning, I woke up early (as I normally do) and grabbed an old, favorite book of mine, *Think and Grow Rich: A Black Choice* by Dr. Dennis Kimbro and Napoleon Hill (author of the original *Think and Grow Rich* book). Dr. Kimbro brilliantly points out that we can transform our life with three magic words: *right mental attitude*.

He eloquently states,

> A right mental attitude is defined as the correct position or bearing in terms of action, feeling, or mood. And it is our actions, feelings, or moods that will determine the actions, feelings, or moods of others toward us. It is our attitude toward life that will determine life's attitude towards us." He supports this statement with, "Our attitude sets the stage for what will occur in our lives – good attitude, good results; fair attitude, fair results; poor attitude, poor results. Each of us shapes his own life; and the shapes of our lives will be and are determined by our attitude. (1991, p. 289)

Those words hit me like a Mike Tyson uppercut.

I read those same words in 1994 and they had the same impact; yet somehow, it was 16 years later and, going through what I had just gone through, I was rejuvenated. The rest of the weekend, I relaxed, spent good quality time with my wife and planned my upcoming work week. Monday was a whole new day for me. I came in well rested, well-dressed, and organized. I was smiling and moving with swag again.

I sent my boss an email requesting a meeting at his earliest convenience. He was out of town, so we met a few days later. When he finally called me to his office, I presented the corrected information that was botched during the staff meeting and said something along these lines: "Mr. (unnamed), I appreciate you allowing me the opportunity to meet with you today and present the updated statistics. I was not prepared for the meeting that day and, for that, I apologize. It is out of my character to show up unprepared and I will ensure this is the last time it will happen." The boss, very unexcited, accepted my apology and thanked me for bringing the correct info. That was my first time taking that approach, and it felt liberating.

My positive attitude was another huge turning point in my approach to my career. Owning my mistakes became more comfortable as I ran into work-related conflicts and challenges. Many of the people whom I've communicated with in my professional networks have shown me tremendous gratitude and respect because I am willing to accept blame, especially if they're among my work teams in subordinate roles. Many years after people have worked under me, I periodically hear kind words and thanks for being a great boss and helpful person. I take great pride in being that way. I was raised well. Thank you, Mom (VK), Grandma Pearlie Mae (R.I.P.), Pop (Vic Johnson), and a slew of siblings, aunties, an uncle, stepmom, and mentors.

I have enjoyed many great relationships in my life and I look forward to so many more! I appreciate the ones that I have and the people who appreciate me. Love you all!

8: PREPARING EVERYTHING FOR MY 1ST RENTAL PROPERTY

Let's go back in my story to Fall 2013 when I was working for Title Masters. You may recall that I mentioned that they had decided to wind down the business. At that time, I was earning about $75,000 per year, my credit score was in the 600 range and I had only $2,500 saved. In general, things were going well, but I knew that I would need a new employer within six to nine months and I needed to start figuring that out. I had a strong network, so there were people telling me to contact them once I had a definite date of my availability to start working elsewhere. There was some momentum building around my initial meetings with Natalie (of EZCORP) but nothing was solid yet. Then, I received that call from EZCORP in October 2013. They invited me to meet with some key executives in their Austin, Texas office. This was the first time that I'd ever been flown into a city for an interview; it felt like I was truly a businessman, which gave me confidence. I bought a suit and briefcase and prepared to meet their team.

When I arrived in Austin, I was intrigued by the airport. Austin is known as "The Live Music Capital of the World," so the airport has a real 'cool vibe' and a couple stages for live bands to perform. The driver took me straight to the interview, while providing details about city monuments and buildings that we passed by. During my first hour in the city, I felt very calm. As nervous as I was for these interviews, once I met the team members, everyone made me feel appreciated. I felt like I was a celebrity coming to the office and they were honored to have me there. Later, I learned that they already decided to hire me; the rest was meeting me in person and convincing me that Austin was where I should relocate my family. On my way back to the airport, they took me to a Tex-Mex restaurant called Torchy's. After eating the chicken fajita taco and cheese dip with my nachos, I told myself, "This could work out." Now, I needed them to properly present the offer.

A couple days later, the recruiter called me with the offer. They made an offer of $90,000/year + 20% annual bonus opportunity (an additional $18,000) for a total 'potential' annual salary of $108,000/year. They also offered a $10,000 relocation allowance. I was super excited. This was the six-figure job that I had prayed and worked hard for.

After researching Austin, comparing cost of living versus Atlanta, and discussing all the options with my wife, we decided that I would first go to Austin to test things out and set up our living situation. Once I started the job on December 13, 2013, I flew Latasha out to tour the city. She loved it! The water, the trees, the peacefulness, and the easy commute were all positives that sold her on the move; plus, once we sold the house in Lithonia, we would be able to pay off the rest of our major debts, save a few bucks, and get my youngest daughter Tai situated until the end of the school year.

This was a big financial turning point for us.

The above image shows summer with the family in Galveston, Texas, June 2014. (Left to right: Wife, Latasha; oldest daughter, D'Gindi; youngest daughter, Tai; next youngest daughter, Jasmine; only son, Jahree and myself.)

Latasha and I sold the house at the end of February 2014 for about $75,000. After paying our realtor her commission, we earned about $20,000 at closing. GLORY TO GOD! With the increased earnings, I was making and this nice profit (after only two and a half years since the purchase), we were starting to see the path to our wealth and true happiness. This also really got me interested in how we could generate more of these money windfalls.

Within a couple of months, my credit score jumped to about 650; my family and I were starting to save about $500/month, maybe closer to $700/month with the 401k contributions I was making. Things were clearly getting better for us; we could see it and feel it. We flew the kids out to Austin in June 2014, drove down to Galveston, Texas, and hung out for Juneteenth weekend. This was a great summer vacation, certainly much better than the ones I hustled together when funds were tight (long drives and short weekends to Myrtle Beach and Orlando, FL in prior summers).

The rest of 2014 was dedicated to saving money, continuing to work on my credit score and being successful at work (so that I could continue the upward trend). My daily habits got more refined and specific. I started focusing on my health and working out more often since I was now 40 years old. Although my family and I were eating out a little more, we were always conscious of what and how much we were consuming. Austin supports very healthy lifestyles; there are always people jogging, cycling, surfing, skateboarding, and walking dogs. There are fit boot camps on every block and so many health food eateries. This was great for Latasha and me, since we could do so much of this together. If we weren't doing something healthy, we were exploring Austin or hitting the road to explore surrounding cities in Central Texas (which is such a beautiful part of the country). We were already living a life of happiness, at least more than we had experienced in our combined lives. When you can pay your bills each month, save money and still have funds left over (even when the next check arrives), it brings a level of comfort to your life. You feel more secure because you know you can handle an emergency when it comes up and still can help others when presented with the opportunity.

LIFE COACH MOMENT

John C. Maxwell wrote: "People cannot do something of significance and stay in their comfort zones at the same time. To do something great, you must take risks."

On the way home from work on an April 2015 afternoon, I tuned into the Jeff Ward radio talk show. An ad ran and said something like, "Do you want to retire within five years? Do you want to generate passive income every month? If so, come to 'whatever hotel' for a one-hour presentation about real estate investing." Hmm, interesting. For years, I'd read about people who purchased single-family homes that needed a little repair, fixed them, then rented them out or sold them for a profit. My grandmother, Margarite Johnson (my dad's mother), purchased rental properties in New York back in the 1960s and 1970s. That was quite amazing for a Black woman during that time. Grandma Pearlie Mae (my mom's mother) also purchased her home in San Francisco back in 1961 for approximately $21,000. At one point in 2008 (before the recession hit us all), her home was worth north of one million dollars. That is an amazing return on an investment! These two ladies (and many other real estate stories I had read and heard of) convinced me that this was going to be the next step in our journey towards financial freedom, wealth, and happiness. Latasha and I went to the one-hour meeting. The speaker, Chris Carrillo, said a few things that instantly resonated with me:

- Measure life by RESULTS, not success or failure.

- Save your pennies.

- Surround yourself with like-minded people.

- There are five ways to make money through real estate investing. (We will dive into this in the next chapter.)

- There are over 5,000 United States tax codes telling you how NOT TO PAY TAXES (many of which are related to real estate).

As he continued, I felt a strong sense of desire. I felt the desire for the financial freedom that many have achieved through real estate investing. It was a way to earn good money and have time to pursue other dreams. This was very inspiring, but extremely frightening. By now, I'd saved about $12,000 and my credit score was still in the 650 range, so I sat there wondering if we had enough money and credit to get into this business.

Chris got to the part of the meeting where he invited you and your partner to come to the two-day real estate investor training. This was a Saturday and Sunday class (seven hours each day) in San Antonio. The class taught participants the step-by-step ways to buy rental property and how to progress as far up the scale as they pleased. The cost came to $500.

Latasha and I looked at each other; even though $500 was not terribly awful for us, at that point in our lives, it felt like we were deciding whether or not to jump off of a cliff. At least to me, the $500 meant that we would have to fully commit our energy into this investment. We walked outside the room, immediately held each other's hands, and said a prayer. We asked God to guide us through this moment, to give us the feeling we were looking for to make such a difficult decision, and to guide and protect us.

Latasha and I gave each other a kiss and decided to 'jump off the cliff' into this exploratory world of real estate investing and becoming landlords. With one swipe of my Chase debit card, we paid $500 and enrolled in the two-day class with Lifestyles Unlimited (http://www. lifestylesunlimited.com/) on Memorial Day weekend. The class also provided 2 years of basic support, a list of vendors that offered discounts on paint, general contracting and other real estate related services. There was also a booklet to refer to and store our class notes.

When I got home, I could not wait to update my vision board and goal board and grab a few recommended books. I also updated my LinkedIn profile to reflect my new career as a real estate investor. With that $500 investment, I considered myself a 'professional real estate investor.' Every day since then, I have carried myself as a professional real estate investor. This allowed my network to treat me as such and attracted other professional real estate investors to me so that I could start consuming as much about this life as possible. During this time, there was a lot of reading and research. I made up my mind that *we would not fail at this.* I had read all the old-school real estate books and seen all the videos (such as Carlton Sheets and others), but I never acted because I allowed my credit and finances to convince me that it was not possible. This time would be different. I removed those fears and obstacles. Basically, I got out of my own way, thus allowing the law of attraction and my determination to drive my wife and me through this process.

So, let's take an account of how my financial picture looked at this point. This will help you gauge my situation and understand how I turned these numbers into a real estate portfolio that went from $0 to $950,000 in three years and three months. Many readers are likely in a much better financial situation than where we started, while others may be nowhere close. Hopefully, the preceding chapters have given you the courage to get your mindset in place to help you 'jump off the cliff' into this exploratory world of real estate investing and becoming landlords.

Victor's Financial Picture as of May 2015	
Annual Income	$110,000/year
Credit Score	650
Debt to Income Ratio:	30%
Savings	$12,000
Properties	0

9: MY 1ST RENTAL PROPERTY DEAL

By now, you have a sense of the changes I made over the years to align myself with success. It started with a focus to advance in a corporate career, which helped my wife and me get out of debt. It also gave me confidence. Through the years, I have prepared for so many interviews and sent so many follow up emails and phone calls; those activities build your character. They taught me how to be an effective communicator. I take great pride in my ability to find a connection with most of the people I meet. Many of these skills were nurtured through these interactions.

My corporate life is a life that I am proud of, but there is a passion that has been inside of me since I was a teenager. I am sure this same passion sits within everyone who reads this book. That passion is to be my own boss, run my own business, and live the dreams that I've envisioned for myself. These dreams include controlling my own time while still making good money. Through all my years of research, one of the main ways people have legally earned great sums of money is through real estate. Therefore, it became time for me to transition my ambition for greater corporate success to a life of passive income streams, primarily real estate.

The Lifestyles Unlimited class was held in San Antonio, which was an hour drive from Austin. Since the classes were starting at 8 a.m. on both days, my wife and I decided to get a room at the Doubletree Hotel, which was close to the location of the class. We love Doubletree because of the warm cookies they give you at check-in. On Saturday morning, we grabbed some breakfast tacos and hot tea and headed to class. There were about 60 other motivated individuals in the room. A highly energetic dude in his mid-40s came to the front of the room. David Fisher is the primary instructor/mentor in the San Antonio and Dallas markets. He was extremely motivating and knowledgeable; he could answer each question with ease, and I was in awe. It was exciting to see someone dropping all this fascinating information on us in a very consumable tone.

I would never use this platform to attempt to teach the Lifestyles Unlimited model, which has been crafted over the past 25 years by its founder, Del Walmsley. Del is a former body builder who started this business in the early 1990s and built a tremendous mentoring program. I will, however, encourage any of my readers who are serious about becoming a real estate investor, to get involved with Lifestyles Unlimited as quickly as possible. Visit their website, www.lifestylesunlimited.com, or contact me through my links so I can get you connected to your nearest location.

However, there is a basic formula that all successful real estate investors use. The formula can be found in any book or Internet video that talks about real estate investing.

Here's an example of the general logic (using hypothetical numbers):

1) Buy a house in a marketable neighborhood that needs repairs. After the repairs, let's say it will be worth $100,000, for the sake of this example.
2) Buy the house for $65,000 (because it needs repairs/renovations).
3) Invest $20,000 to complete the repairs/renovations.
4) The total investment will amount to $85,000.
5) **The equity (profit) earned after repairs will amount to $15,000**. Equity is the difference in the current value (after repaired value) and what you spent (or what you owe if you have a mortgage.)

The home value after repairs will amount to $100,000 minus the total investment, including purchase and repairs, which will amount to $85,000.

If sold or refinanced, the total equity/potential profit will amount to $15,000 ($100k - $85k = $15k).

If this were the scenario (and if the investor decided to sell the property or refinance it), they would earn about $15,000 (less if there were any closing costs associated with selling or refinancing). There are dozens of strategies that will drastically alter this outcome in each direction, but we'll talk about that another time.

Getting Started in This Business

By that Sunday afternoon, our minds were blown. We had enough information to at least take the steps to get into our first rental property deal. The plan was to buy a small house in San

Antonio, Texas at a discounted rate and then rent it out to a hard-working family. We chose San Antonio because it was a thriving city with a large military population and plenty of jobs. We lived in Austin at the time, so we were just close enough to get there within an hour to manage the property. I figured if we could find a property that cost $90,000 or less, we would only have an all-in monthly payment on the house of about $600 per month.

In the areas that we targeted, the average rent ranged from $900 per month to $1,100 per month. That meant a monthly profit of $300 - $500 per month. That was sweet on top of my normal paycheck! We are talking about a potential extra $6,000 per year. To some folks, that's nothing, but that could do a lot for my family and me. It could pay a car note or cover groceries for a month. It could pay for a couple utility bills plus gas for our vehicles for a month. We could also just save it and let it accumulate interest so that we could have money to buy another house one day. This would also be a great way to help a family potentially upgrade their living situation by renting them a freshly renovated home.

Goal: Buy a single-family property for $90,000 or less by August 31, 2015 (three months since the class) and have a tenant in it by October 1, 2015.

With our goal in mind, it was now time to apply the knowledge we gained over the weekend, so we could see this goal through. We would need a way to finance the purchase of the property and give us a few dollars to repair it. Many conventional mortgage lenders will not provide you with rehab money, therefore, many real estate investors use private lenders or hard money lenders. Hard Money Lenders (HMLs) are lenders who finance the purchase of an investment property if it meets certain criteria; they also provide the funds to rehab the property. However, they charge a much higher interest rate than a conventional lender.

The HML may charge in the 15% range, while the conventional lender would hover around 4½% to 5% (as of this writing). We could do a whole chapter on this, but one of the benefits of using an HML is that your credit is not their concern; they want to ensure that the property value increases after its rehabilitation. If you do not make the payments, they assume the property. The other benefit of using an HML is that it's just like using cash regarding making an offer on the property. They can close on properties much faster than traditional banks and mortgage companies because there is much less underwriting. If a bank would take 30 days to close, an HML could close in two weeks.

The smart real estate investors will use hard money to purchase an investment property, rehab the property as quickly as possible, and refinance the property through a conventional lender. Since the property was purchased at a discount due to the repairs needed, its value has increased, and it should now match the value of the nicer homes on the block. The conventional lender pays off the hard money lenders' note, but since the property's value has increased, you receive money back at the closing table.

There are several ways to acquire financing for investment property purchases and rehabs. Below are a few options that you can research.

- Conventional Lenders

- Hard Money Lenders
- Savings (Cash)
- Refinance Your Primary Residence
- 401k/IRA Accounts
- Personal Loan (Family, Friends, etc.)
- Private Lenders/Investors
- Assume Ownership (Subject-To)
- Tax Lien Auctions
- Inheritance
- Real Estate Investment Trusts

"People often ask me which creative real estate techniques I would recommend they use when purchasing property. While I would like to give them a magic answer, the truth is, that the best real estate techniques are the ones YOU DEVELOP that work best for you. As a matter of fact, some of my most profitable transactions were made possible by combining techniques." —Carlton Sheets (*Becoming a Real Estate Investor*)

The evening after I left the Lifestyles Unlimited class, I started looking for a conventional mortgage lender that I could work with to get preapproved for a conventional mortgage; I would not use this lender initially, but I needed to know if I could get approved for a conventional mortgage in order to refinance a property later.

I found a mortgage lender and my 650-credit score, combined with my income and savings, happened to be strong enough for them to preapprove me for a loan. The lender emailed me a preapproval letter. This would be used as evidence that I could get financing to purchase a home when I submitted offers on properties that I wanted to purchase.

Now it was time for my wife and I to search for the perfect investment property. We knew our criteria and knew the area that would work for us. This was another scary part of the process; if we picked the wrong house, we could pay too much for repairs or end up having a hard time renting it out. We found a realtor who was very familiar with the area and had previously worked with investors. Finding a realtor who understood what I was trying to accomplish was important to me. As an investor, this was not a home that I was moving my family into; it was more of a first-time buyer home. The search began.

The property that we were pursuing would need repairs. We wanted a home that needed repairs because these properties would be less expensive than ones in the neighborhood with a similar structure and size, but better conditions. These properties are called COMPARABLES or COMPS.

LIFE COACH MOMENT

CMA (Comparable Market Analysis) or Comparables, more popularly known as Comps – this is the practice of comparing the value of like and kind single-family properties and taking the average between them.

Real estate investors heavily use COMPS to determine if the price for the investment property will work for them. If the price of the considered house was $100,000 and needed $20,000 worth of repairs, that meant the investment would be a total of $120,000. If the other homes on that block (the Comps) were selling for $110,000, then an investor would be walking into that deal with a potential $10,000 loss if the COMPS were calculated properly. Spending $120k for a house worth $110k is hustling backwards. Therefore, prudent real estate investors ensure that they have reliable sources to gather accurate Comps before making an offer on a property. A licensed realtor can access this information through the multi-listing service (MLS).

An MLS is a marketing database that is set up by a group of cooperating real estate brokers. Its purpose is to provide accurate and structured data about properties for sale. It's also a mechanism for listing brokers to offer compensation to buyer brokers who bring a buyer for their listed property. (Reference: https://www.thebalancesmb.com/multiple-listing-services-in-real-estate-2866909)

We drove down to San Antonio every weekend for the next three weeks and probably saw 25 houses. Some were in the right location yet required too many repairs; others only required simple paint jobs but were not in the best neighborhoods. We found one property that fit our wish list; the price for this home was $85,000. I sent our realtor a copy of the preapproval letter from my lender, and he submitted an offer to the seller's realtor. If the seller accepted the offer, we would need to have earnest money ready. Earnest money is a good faith deposit that represents your intention to move forward with the purchase. That amount was 1% or $850 if the offer was accepted. This was exciting and nerve-wracking. The realtor called me after a few days and said, "Hello, Mr. Johnson. Unfortunately, the seller accepted another offer." Latasha and I were disheartened, but we continued the search. We were online every chance we got, looking for this first property. After a month (since we did not have an exclusivity clause with the realtor), we ended up finding another realtor. This time, we came across a guy named Shawn Trejo. Shawn is a licensed real estate agent, but his full-time job was as a firefighter in the Houston area. Shawn immediately began sending us listings in our target area that met our wish list. After the first couple of days, we found one that was almost exactly what we wanted. One of our main requirements was for the listing to have three bedrooms, two bathrooms, with a two-car garage. The provided listing had three bedrooms, one bathroom, and a one-car garage. We ran the numbers to see if this listing would fit into our investment strategy, and it did.

We sent Shawn the pre-approval letter and he submitted the offer at $84,000, which was also the asking price by the bank. That happened on July 8, 2015. This house was being sold by the bank as a foreclosed house and was vacant for several months.

LIFE COACH MOMENT

A foreclosure is a home that belongs to the bank, which once belonged to a homeowner. The homeowner either abandoned the home or voluntarily deeded the home to the bank.

In fact, the previous owner also abandoned their dog in the home. The dog ended up stuck in the house for several weeks and was unattended to. It destroyed the place in an effort to get free. Eventually, the authorities rescued the dog. I never found out what happened to the dog. Anyway, the place was left in shambles: holes in the walls, sheetrock torn apart, floors scratched and chipped and feces everywhere. Oh yeah, real estate investing can be a nasty and dirty job.

You must be able to use those visualization skills in order to see the future potential of the property. The skill is being able to make the property nice, clean, and safe without going overboard with the rehab. Many inexperienced real estate investors will make the mistake of buying granite countertops, chandeliers, and the works, when all they need is to fix the major issues like HVAC, plumbing, floors, painting throughout, landscaping, and a good clean up. Obviously, each home is different, but the point is to get the property clean, safe, and comfortable for the market.

It took about a week for us to hear back on this deal, but when Shawn called, he said, "Hey Vic, they accepted the offer at $82,400." We were overjoyed and thankful. It felt just like the offer that was accepted on our first home in Lithonia, except this one felt different because it was a business venture. My wife and I conquered our fears and 'jumped off the cliff.' I sent Shawn an earnest money check for $824 (1%), which also allowed us a seven-day option period. The 'option period' is an agreed upon amount of time that the buyer must use to inspect the property and make a final decision about going forward with the purchase of the property. If there are extensive repairs beyond the buyer's threshold of tolerance and affordability, they can walk away with no penalty and get the earnest money back. No harm, no foul.

We found an inspection company and paid them about $325 to inspect the ins and outs of the house. When the report came back, some of the main items that required attention were holes in the walls that needed sheetrock repair and painting, carpet in the bedrooms, an off-track garage door, a bathtub that needed resurfacing, kitchen cabinets in need of refurbishing, appliances that needed to be replaced, landscaping, and a few of the planks in the fence that required repair. The place also needed simple touch-ups to give it a fresh look. The main items that would have made us walk away (especially since we only had $7,000 to close on the house and $5,000 for repairs) would have been things like roof damage, major plumbing issues, A/C and heating system issues, electrical issues, or foundation issues. These are the *big repairs* that can put a huge dent in your investment plans. Since the big repairs were listed as 'ok' or 'no concern,' we decided to go forward with the purchase.

The BIG VACATION to California

During the Summer of 2015, I took the opportunity to do something that I wanted to do for the prior 20 years: take all my biological children (D'Gindi, Jahree, and Jasmine) and now my wife and stepdaughter, Tai, to see my grandmother, Pearlie Mae (at the time, she was the matriarch of my family). Now that the house was officially under contract, I could handle much of the dealings via cellphone and emails, at least until I got back in about 10 days. This was truly a monumental moment for me. By 1996 and at the age of 22, I had three kids by two different mothers and funds were hard to come by. The family I grew up with were all in the Bay Area of California, and I was living in Atlanta when my kids were born. It was one of my desires to have enough resources to take all three children to California to meet the other half of their family.

While I was in California, I was still handling business like a pro. Now was time for the real work of locking in the financing, but I could not use the conventional lender that preapproved us because this house had too much rehab to be done. I decided to go with a hard money lender, InvestMark. This proved to be the best decision for my wife and me at the time. We were fortunate to connect with a guy named Joey Sullivan. He and his wife Natalie were extremely helpful for us during this first deal. They were patient, informative, knowledgeable, and, most of all, available when we needed quick answers.

They went well outside the bounds of being lenders to us; they were mentors. They are also real estate investors. Through Joey, I learned about a local group in Austin called Homes for the Win. This is another husband and wife team of real estate investors, Andrew and Linda Pederson. This couple will buy an investment property and then invite other investors to come to the house as they decide on what rehab to do, what things not to do, and how to negotiate with contractors and collect license and insurance information from them.

Latasha and I went to a few of these and saved thousands of dollars from the lessons taught by Andrew and Linda. They probably would not remember us, but they impacted me enough to mention them in this book. If you are in the Austin area and just getting into real estate investing, check them out. When you are in this process, you want to absorb as much information from as many successful people as possible.

Don't be afraid to ask questions; people realize that we all started somewhere. I, certainly, was not shy about speaking to people who were taking action in this business, and, in most cases, I have not been steered wrong. Doing more in-depth research if someone shared a tip with me was key. If there was a meet-up happening somewhere, and they were discussing real estate, I would bring a list of compiled questions and strike up a conversation with someone else in the room. You never know what you will learn, who you will meet, and where that relationship could take you in the future. It can be challenging to network and meet new people, but if that is the biggest obstacle blocking you from wealth and happiness, you'd better find a way to conquer it. It is necessary in all business.

We were still on vacation in San Francisco and the time difference was my friend. The family would sleep until 10 a.m. PST (which was 12 p.m. CT), so I would get up around 7 a.m. PST (9 a.m. CST) and make calls to vendors to get quotes for repairs on the house, email documents to InvestMark (to ensure financing was going as scheduled), call Shawn to coordinate things that he needed, etc. I was so busy making things happen with the house that I didn't have time to be afraid of us failing. It was like FEAR had left because it was not getting any of my attention. There was too much work to be done for me to pause and let FEAR have a say in any of this. Not only that, with every conversation I had with a vendor, Joey, Shawn, or a Lifestyles Unlimited member, my knowledge and confidence increased. I FELT BIGGER! I felt like a professional real estate investor.

By now, we were in the last few days of July and the last two days of our California Vacation. I received a call from my boss, LeighAnn. I love that lady, even to this day. Anyway, she called me and didn't sound like her normal, energetic self. "Hey LeighAnn, how are you?" I asked. "I'm fine, Victor. I am so sorry to bother you while on vacation, but when are you coming back?" she asked. I replied, "We fly out tomorrow and I am back the day after. Is everything okay?" LeighAnn was definitely not comfortable and responded, "Well, buddy, I need to talk to you, but we need to meet face-to-face. Call me when you are on the way to the office in two days, and we will meet at Starbucks." LeighAnn had worked with me for a year and a half at that point and knew damn well I am not a Starbucks fan. I knew something was up. I responded, "Okay, LeighAnn. I'll see you in a couple days."

This call didn't really frazzle me like I thought it would; I gained maturity by mastering my mindset over the prior few years. However, I was curious, so I ran through a couple of scenarios in my head.

1) Was I being transferred to a different area of the business?

2) We did get a new CEO; was there a big change coming?

Either way, I knew it was going to work out for me because my business units' numbers were consistently outperforming our historical numbers. With that, I decided to block it out for two days and enjoy this last full day in the Bay. We enjoyed food, folks, cards, laughs, pictures, and fun.

Periodically, I would catch Pearlie Mae sitting in her chair in the middle of the room, gazing at all of her descendants with pride. A smile, a laugh, a comment; it was beautiful to see. In that moment, I THANKED GOD FOR BLESSING ME WITH THE OPPORTUNITY TO MAKE THAT MOMENT HAPPEN (for her and for myself). She was 91 years old during that trip. Three years later, we would lose Pearlie Mae Anderson at the age of 93. I love you, Pearlie Mae!!!

The 'Big Vacation to California' came to an end and the kids safely made it home to Atlanta. Latasha, Tai, and I were back in Austin and it was the end of July. By now, we had an official closing date scheduled (August 20, 2015) and it was back to work. As promised, I called LeighAnn before I headed to work that morning and she invited me to the Starbucks near the office. We briefly embraced and sat down with our orders. She got straight to the point. "They have decided to discontinue the loan side of the EZCORP business, which includes the Auto Lending and Pay Day Divisions (us). They are going to issue the full severance, plus a retention bonus to those who are part of the shutdown team (us)," she stated. My reply was, "Well, that is a mouthful. I have two questions: 1) How long is my retention period, if accepted, and 2) How much is the total package?"

They were offering me a package that totaled $30,000 if I stayed through 11/30/2015 (four months), in addition to my normal salary and bonuses until closure.

This was basically three months' salary for me, and it included a few other perks such as a career transition team to help with resumes and interview skills. This was a fabulous offering, especially for many of the team members who were not receiving packages at that level. There was another great perk for me in this deal. Suddenly, my work load decreased, which allowed me to have more time on my hands. The timing could not be better. Many of the remaining management team were starting to work half days so they could network and interview for their next jobs. I used my time to deal with this rental property. I was just getting to the crucial part of the loan process. Over the course of the final three weeks until closing (and even the next two weeks while rehab was being completed) I drove to San Antonio at least 20 times (about four times per week). This would not have been possible prior to the company deciding to shut down my business division. This is a prime example of why we must stay positive while focusing on what we want in life; we have no foresight into all the events that will shape our outcomes. This is what I mean when I say, "God and the Universe will take care of the rest." Had someone asked me three months prior if I wanted to get laid off from my six-figure job, I would have responded, "Hell No!" My simple mind would not have assumed that there would be a severance package and extra time off to handle personal affairs.

There were several things that I needed to do during these last weeks and prior to closing on the rental property. Below is a checklist of things I focused on:

- Getting an umbrella insurance coverage quote
- Order a property appraisal
- Send my hard money lender the documentation (Many of the county and property related documents they were able to assist with, like property survey and appraisal.)
- Prepare a scope of work (a detailed description of all the rehab work that I wanted done: exact brands of ceiling fans, facets, paint colors, etc.)
- Get three separate rehab bids from different contractors using the same scope of work in order to compare pricing for the work that is needed so my hard money lender could determine what the finished product would look like and compare it to the COMPS in the area. It is then used to value the property and ultimately determine the loan amount that they're comfortable with. In my situation, they loaned $87,000 (which covered $82,400 purchase price and gave $4,600 towards repairs). This helped tremendously because I ended up spending about $10,000 on all the rehab; they covered about half of it through the loan. It's always great to lower your out-

of-pocket costs, especially when you have less cash to work with.

- Take pictures of the property before the rehab started so you can compare before & after improvements and start building a catalogue.
- Research rental prices in the area to begin marketing the property immediately after closing.

We'd done our rental COMPS, but now we actually knew the rehab we were getting done, so we could really dial in. You may be wondering why we would start marketing before closing, especially since we can't start rehab until we own the property. Well, one of the great lessons we learned through Lifestyles Unlimited is that you want to put your 'FOR RENT' sign in the yard as soon as you leave the closing table. You can always list 'Available on x/x/xxxx- Newly Renovated.' Potential renters love to rent a place that has been cleaned up just before moving in.

It is also important to note that I did not neglect my responsibilities at work. I had a lighter load than before, but there were still duties to fulfill and a business to run until the lights were off. The atmosphere in the office was a mixture of joy, sadness, stress, and excitement; it just depended upon people's attitudes. The largest group of employees were leaving 30 days from the announcement of the closure. Then, another group phased out at 60 days, then 90 days, until the last month when there was only 10% of the staff left. Those days were weird. The remaining staff were more tenured employees; therefore, the work environment resembled a small office of leaders who came to do their thing while locking in their next jobs and bringing in lunch mostly every day.

The Closing and Becoming Landlords

Chirping was what I heard outside our bedroom window around 6:30 a.m. on Thursday, August 20, 2015, our closing day! Both Latasha and I realized what today meant for us. We had confronted our debts. We changed our mindset about money. We remained positive. We set goals and accomplished many of them through our mindset changes. We changed our daily habits to attract more of what we wanted. We maintained great health. We acted 'as if' we were real estate investors and became just that. We prayed a lot. We saved a little money. We improved our credit. We confronted our fears! But most importantly, *we took action*. And by 2:28 p.m., I was the proud owner of our first investment property! It was a great moment in our lives.

That evening, my wife and I immediately listed the property on Craigslist and a few other sites. Within three days, we had five prospective tenants contact us. We scheduled a showing of the property and drove back down to San Antonio. We gathered applications and other required documents and found a screening service through TransUnion that would give us background info, criminal info, and credit info. We followed all Texas landlord/tenant laws. TransUnion also provided a recommendation based on the combined screening information, which included things like: 'Recommendation: Decline-Previous Eviction,' or 'Recommendation: Accept.' Ultimately, it was our decision as the owners, but this service was extremely helpful, especially in the beginning. After receiving three unfavorable applications, we found one for a young family, with two kids. The husband and wife were working decent jobs enough to cover three times the rent, and they really liked the house and the area, since it was close to their parents. We approved their application and they moved in at the end of September 2015 once the rehab was completed.

While we were marketing and showing the property during the rehab, accepting applications, screening applicants, and accepting an applicant, I was managing the final phases of the rehab work. Things were going smooth for the most part; I had to make a few modifications along the way for various reasons, but Latasha and I were able to stay close to the budget. The crew was paid on time every week, upon completion of different parts of labor, and everyone was happy at the end of the day. I even used the crew again when the first tenants moved out and before the second tenant moved in. By October 1, 2015, we had the property purchased, rehabbed, and leased.

We were still under the hard money loan and it would end up taking a few extra months to refinance. Unfortunately, in the three months since I received the preapproval letter, my credit score moved down ever so slightly but enough to cause a delayed approval. I ended up going through one of the best real estate investor mortgage lender entities in Texas, AMP Lending.

I worked with a great guy named Rich Nunez. He walked Latasha and me through the best steps to get the property refinanced under a more affordable loan. The hard money loan was costing us $1,100 per month; we were collecting rent of $1,100 per month, so we earned no profit until we refinanced. Once Rich was able to get us refinanced through AMP Lending, our total monthly payment went down to $580 per month; we immediately started making a monthly cash flow profit of $520 per month. That went on for the next two years, until we sold Branching Peak in the fall of 2017. We never had a tenant pay more than a few days late and we never had to evict anyone. Latasha and I provided a safe and comfortable residence for two young families, while also helping us become more financially secure.

Branching Peak by the Numbers

Purchase Price (lender paid)	$82,400
Rehab costs (lender paid 1/2)	$10,000
Closing costs (purchase & refinance)	$5,000
TOTAL OUT OF POCKET COSTS	$15,000
Rent collected (2+ years)	$26,400
Mortgage payments (2+ years)	$16,000
CASH FLOW PROFIT (2+ YEARS)	$10,600
Nov. 2017 property sold amount	$128,500
Less loan payoff & closing costs	$95,000
Cash received at sale	$33,000
TOTAL CASH RETURN	$43,400
TOTAL OUT OF POCKET	$15,000
NET RETURN ON INVESTMENT	289%

Real estate offers so many ways to become financially free, wealthy, and happy. It was amazing for us to see this all come to fruition. Even before we sold the property, my wife and I were seeing the benefits of the extra cash flow that was coming into our home. We were saving more. There were a few more dinners out on the town, but that was manageable. The main thing we had to do was continue to watch our expenses, manage our credit by paying all the bills on time, prepare Tai for college, and save to invest so we could continue growing our wealth and the portfolio. Each house brings us closer to financial freedom where we can decide if we want to continue the traditional corporate life.

Additionally, we always seek out opportunities to help others. It could be as simple as introducing someone to a connection that could help them or providing some form of information that helps someone level up. This is the main reason I decided to write this book. Through my journey, someone out there will be inspired to take action towards accomplishing their goals. If any or all of the information provided in this book can help that person achieve wealth, good health, success, and happiness, then I will be satisfied with this work. My story is one about an ordinary person who pushed through many obstacles to achieve extraordinary heights, and I am very thankful and humbled by it.

CONCLUSION

It turned out that fall 2015 was another 'turning point' for Latasha and me. By December 2015, we were two months into tenants moving into the rental property and I received the $30,000 severance and retention bonus. There was a small part of me that wanted to take off for a couple months and pretend to be a full-time real estate investor, but I needed to immediately find a job so that we did not fall back into where we were at the end of 2010 when I was laid off due to corporate shutdown.

Through my former colleague, Debra Tucker from my Mann Bracken days, I was able to land a new gig with a small debt purchasing firm. They bought charged off debt and outsourced most of it to collection law firms. My role was to stay abreast of all of the collection regulations and draft policies and procedures for the collection law firms to adhere to. From there, I would schedule onsite audits at their locations to ensure operation compliance. This caused me to travel a lot during 2016 and early 2017. It was not a bad gig and gave me a chance to work for a day or two in cities like Seattle, Atlanta, Chicago, St. Louis, etc. I was only making about 75% of my previous salary, but it was a convenient location to my home. My debts were lower than when I started at EZCORP, and I had a good team working with me at this new company.

During the entire time we were buying the rental property and during my work at EZCORP, we were still living in an apartment in Austin. So, by mid-2016, Latasha and I decided to buy a primary residence in a city called Kyle, Texas. Kyle is about 30 minutes south of Austin and 45 minutes north of San Antonio. This is the type of home that we always wanted even when we were living in Atlanta. We could now afford to purchase a 4-bedroom, 2 1/2-bathroom home with a fenced in backyard and 2-car garage.

Tai was graduating from high school and headed for college. This left Tasha and I as 'empty-nesters' by Fall 2016. I was 42 and Latasha was younger than me. For most people, this is the ultimate life: we had the home we wanted, vehicles we wanted, our kids were out of high school doing their own thing, and our combined income – including cash flow on the rental–was more than enough to pay all the bills each month, save, and play a little. That just was not enough for me. It felt like we could be doing so much more, so I started researching as many passive income strategies as I could. Things like buying vending machines, investing in dividend stocks, AirBnB, blogging, writing, you name it. Latasha knew I wanted to get involved with some kind of project that could help both of us retire from our traditional work while affording us the opportunity to grow our real estate portfolio. Both of us were still reading, researching a lot, and educating ourselves on real estate and what markets were trending higher with rentals over home purchases. I started focusing on generating enough passive income to cover our monthly expenses.

This was the period when I heard back from Natalie Lampis (who had helped me get the job at EZCORP and was our realtor for the house we were living in). As stated earlier in the book, I ended up accepting the job in Dallas by June 2017. My logic was to buy a house in the Dallas area and only pay a 3.5% down payment since it would be considered a second home. Investment properties typically require a 20% down payment, so buying a second home with a 3.5% down payment would be a great way to add another property to the portfolio with minimal cash out of pocket. This job put me back in the six-digits, plus bonus and relocation costs. Latasha and I agreed that I would set up in Dallas for a few months, while she managed the house in Kyle, and since Tai had come back to Austin, Latasha could be there with her. My son Jahree also moved to Dallas with me for a change of pace from his Atlanta life. In October 2017, we bought a townhouse in North Dallas, and ended up renting out the Kyle house to a great, stable family. As of this writing, it is Summer 2018, and it has been three-years since we purchased our first rental.

During that period, we were very disciplined in applying all of the tools that I have laid out within these pages, and we saved quite a bit of money. The one thing about saving is that it only helps you if you are using the funds for growth or for a necessity. Latasha and I were investing into a couple of stocks during this time and I was putting away about 10% in my 401k plans between all these jobs. Stocks and 401k bring 'compounding interest.'

What is 'Compound Interest?

Compound interest (or compounding interest) is interest calculated on the initial principal and on the accumulated interest of previous periods of deposit or loan. Thought to have originated in 17th century Italy, compound interest can be thought of as "interest on interest," and will make a sum grow at a faster rate than simple interest, which is calculated only on the principal amount. According to Investopedia.

This multiplied the money we put into the stocks. This is not my area of expertise, but I continue reading about it, since I see the benefits of investing in some dividend stocks. Having these funds tucked away has allowed us to continue the empire building. We are purchasing more single-family rental properties, and, at some point, we would love to move up to investing in multi-family properties. One thing that I have realized is that I enjoy striving for larger goals. It excites me to look at something in the beginning with hesitation and fear, then to overcome it through persistent self-belief and faith in God. I have grown so much as a man and I look forward to what God has in store for me on the next leg of this journey.

Victor's Financial Picture as of August 2018	
Annual W-2 Income	Over $100,000/year
Annual Rental Income	$65,400/year
Credit Score	767
Debt to Income Ratio	15%
Properties	4 Rentals/1 Primary Total Value $920,000
Other Investments	Dividend Stocks 17% Contribution to Company 401k 1 Paid for Vehicle

ACKNOWLEDGEMENTS

As of the writing of this book, it is August 2018. I am 44 and a half years old and married to a beautiful woman, inside and out. My children are now 20, 22, 23, 26. They are healthy and safe. They all have their own dreams that they are chasing, and they have my support. I am healthy and in good physical condition, with a sound mind, comfortable home, and friends and family around the world who love me. I AM HAPPY! We have achieved a state of financial comfort that allows us to be free if we were to choose. Therefore, we are WEALTHY.

The name of this book is: *Proven Pathways to Wealth & Happiness!* If you apply the state of mind that I used to achieve my goals, you should also find wealth and happiness. You do not have to do the exact things that I did (although they will help greatly), but I would recommend that you apply the same ENERGY, ENTHUSIASM & PASSION that I applied when going after my goals. I would like to THANK YOU for taking the time to read (or listen) to this book. My prayer is that you find positive results from the words that I have written. TAKE ACTION AND HAVE THE LIFE THAT YOU WANT!

Here is a personal 'thank you' to so many (and don't trip if you don't see your name; blame it on my mind, not on my heart): Latasha Michelle Johnson, my beautiful, intelligent, and supportive wife. Thank you for believing in the crazy dreams that I bring to you. I am glad that a few of them worked. Let's keep thriving, loving, and helping.

I love you! Mother, Valerie Kay Lewis, you are my partner from day one. We have traveled the world on the backs of your hustle. It had its ups and downs, but I have learned so much from your undying love.

Thank You and I love you. Pop, Ernest Vic Johnson- I love you, man. God allowed us to spend close time together from the age of 16 forward, and that was a critical blessing for me. You took me from the boy who thought he was a man to a true man. Thank you for your wisdom, listening ear, and support.

I cannot thank my dad, without also thanking my step-mother, Verla Johnson, for more than 40 years of love and support towards me. Verla 'G-Mama,' you have always shown me love, even when I didn't understand the delivery; it made me stronger, and for that, I am appreciative.

All of my sisters have been important to my life in some form or fashion and I love you all. Thank you and I love you (in no particular order) Ronna, Annelle, Dionne, Ebony, and Ricka. To my cool brothers: Michael, Tayari, & Delon, I love you dudes.

Thank you to the Lifestyles Unlimited Team, especially Del Walmsley, David Fisher, and Joe Flores. There are so many family members, friends, and mentors that I could mention here: thank you!

References

Holodny, E. (2017). The US is creating millionaires faster than anywhere in the world — but it's not as impressive as it sounds *Business Insider.* Retrieved from https://www.businessinsider .com/us-millionaires-growing-faster-than-anywhere-in-world-2017-11

Hurst, K. (n.d.). 6 science facts that prove that the law of attraction exists. Retrieved from http://www .thelawofattraction.com/six-things-need-know-science-behind-law-attraction/.

Spector, N. (2017). Smiling can trick your brain into happiness and boost your health. Retrieved from https://www.nbcnews .com/better/health/smiling-can-trick-your-brain-happiness-boost-your-health-ncna822591

Kimbro D., & Hill, N. (1991). *Think and grow rich: A Black choice,* New York, NY: Fawcett Books.

(R) Pearlie Mae with mom and son at table

(Left to right): V.K. (Mom), Jahree (son), Tai (stepdaughter), D'Gindi (daughter), Jasmine (daughter) Front: Pearlie Mae (Grandma) R.I.P. (7/6/1924 – 11/28/2017) GONE BUT NOT FORGOTTEN!

WINNING!!!!!

SAMPLE PREAPPROVAL LETTER

Conditional Qualification Letter

Date:	6/5/15
Prospective Applicant:	Victor Johnson
Prospective Co-Applicant:	
Address:	TBD
	San Antonio, TX area
Purchase price:	$150,000
Loan amount:	$120,000
Qualifying Interest Rate:	4.5%
Term:	360 months/30 years
Loan-to-Value Ratio:	80%
Loan Type and Description:	Fixed Rate Conventional
Secondary Financing (If applicable):	N/A
Combined LTV:	

********PLEASE ALLOW 30 DAYS FOR CLOSING ********

Residential Mortgage Loan Originator **XX has not** received a signed application for the Loan from the Applicant.

Residential Mortgage Loan Originator **XX has** reviewed the Prospective Applicant's credit reports.

Residential Mortgage Loan Originator **XX has** reviewed the prospective applicant's credit scores.

Residential Mortgage Loan Originator **XX has not received** the prospective applicants' tax returns.

Residential Mortgage Loan Originator **XX has not received** income, debt, and asset related documents.

Based on the information that the Prospective Applicant has provided to the Mortgage Loan Officer, as described above, the Mortgage Loan Officer has determined that the Prospective Applicant is eligible and qualified to meet the financial requirements of the Loan.

This is not an approval for the Loan. Approval of the Loan requires: (1) the residential mortgage loan originator to verify the information that the prospective applicant has provided; (2) the prospective applicant's financial status and credit report to remain substantially the same until the loan closes; (3) the collateral for the loan (the subject property) to satisfy the lender's requirements (for example, appraisal, title, survey, condition, and insurance); (4) the loan, as described, to remain available in the market; (5) the prospective applicant to execute loan documents the lender requires; and (6) the following additional items (list): Loan Approval is subject to IRS INCOME TAX RETURN Validation through Form 4506T

Other documents required for loan approval:

Receipted, Executed purchase agreement

ABOUT THE AUTHOR

Victor Vonico Johnson is a husband, father, motivational mentor to many and real estate investor with over $1,000,000 in single-family rental property throughout Texas, Kansas, and Georgia. He is a published author and influencer, and the Senior Managing Partner of 555 Equity, LLC, a real estate investing and property management company. In his corporate life, he has served as a General Manager & Director of Call Centers and he has mentored dozens within the Collections, Customer Service and Compliance industries, from Georgia to Texas over a 21-year career. Victor has managed the R&B Soul singing duo, Slick & Rose, and Executive Produced their debut album, "Objects in the Mirror" released in 2003, while also hosting radio shows, open mics, talent events and community showcase television shows in his colorful career. He aspires to continue motivating and mentoring people from all walks of life, to help them find love, peace, happiness, and financial freedom in their lives.

54054433R00067

Made in the USA
Columbia, SC
25 March 2019